Human Communications

Third Edition

Stuart Harris

NCC Blackwell
MANCHESTER • OXFORD

British Library Cataloguing in Publication Data
Harris, Stuart

Human Communications — 3rd Ed.
I. Title
658.45
ISBN: 1-85554-207-2

First published in 1987 as *People and Communication*
Second Edition published in 1990 by:

NCC Blackwell Limited, 108 Cowley Road, Oxford OX4 1JF, England.

Third Edition 1993.

Editorial office: The National Computing Centre Limited, Oxford House, Oxford Road, Manchester M1 7ED, England.

Typeset in Palatino/Futura by Wordshop, St Dennis, Cornwall
Printed by Chong Moh Offset Printing Pte. Ltd. Singapore

Preface

INTRODUCTION

This course book is designed to provide students with the necessary written and oral communication skills to enable them to interpret and write documents relevant to today's business world. Parts of the course are suited to formal exposition, but the majority of the unit objectives require that students exercise their communication skills individually and in groups. Students achieve the aims of the course through an integrated approach by dividing the unit into four broad areas:

— gathering, processing and transmitting information

— internal communication within organisations

— working in groups

— individual research.

STAFFING

It is important that the course is not regarded as being similar to a traditional English language course. While the development of self-expression and interpretative skills are valuable, the emphasis here is on group interaction, personal development and oral skills, as well as on looking at the communications process within and between firms. In particular, some role-play situations may test the communication and persuasive skills of the lecturer even more than the students, especially if some of the students happen to be lacking in confidence or motivation.

STUDENTS

The course assumes no particular age group or relevant experience, though the student should be competent in the use of the English language.

EXERCISES

At the end of most chapters are sample questions from past NCC Threshold/Diploma examination papers. In all cases there are no totally correct answers, rather use these questions as a basis for careful discussion after first attempting them. After all, discussion is so important in human communication!

NOTE FOR STUDENTS

By the end of this course, we hope we have:

— Increased your effectiveness in work situations, through the development of language and social skills.

— Contributed to your personal development, by fostering the ability to communicate with and relate to others as individuals, in groups and within organisations.

— Developed your skills in dealing with information in various forms, so that you are better able to acquire, evaluate and organise it for your own purposes, and to present it in an effective form when required, in study and in employment.

— Encouraged in you a sensitivity to the ideas and attitudes of others, an awareness of how these can be effected by you and other people, and a willingness to adapt to them where necessary.

S Harris

Acknowledgements

The author wishes to acknowledge the following people for their contribution to the publication of this book:
Thanks are due to Mr George Penney, who edited the original text.
Also, for additional material supplied, the author is grateful to Mary Graham and Jenny Rice.
Case study: *Esther Boswell processes words* used with kind permission of Eric Deeson, from *Computing and information technology*, Blackwell, 1988.

Contents

1 Introduction to communication

OBJECTIVES

When you have worked through this chapter, you will be able to:

- state what we mean by human communication
- list some barriers to communication in different contexts
- comment on the importance of language to human communication
- list some techniques of communication and their value
- list some ways in which people may abuse communication
- describe the significance of feedback
- list some of the ways the sender of a message may improve communication
- list some of the ways the receiver may improve communication.

INTRODUCTION

Throughout this book we will be considering the process of communication – a process which most people never think about analytically. In fact this is often the cause of breakdowns in communication, or of manipulation and abuse of the receivers. Those who do analyse the use of the communication process gain an unusual insight into human nature. We will start with some basic concepts.

1.1 WHAT IS COMMUNICATION?

At the centre of any definition of communication (see Figure 1.1) must be the intention of conveying a message, even if the message is abstract (modern poetry, for example). The message may not be intended for anybody in particular and may be simply for the enjoyment of the creator: so there may be no intended receiver.

There will always be a transmitter in a communication but a message is usually both transmitted and received (see Figure 1.2), though some messages may not reach their destination if there is a barrier to communication. Such a barrier may vary from a reception problem with your radio or television, to a listener whose mind is on other things or who does not understand the message. It is important, therefore, to convey a message via the best possible medium or through a combination of media ie face-to-face, via the telephone or in a written communication.

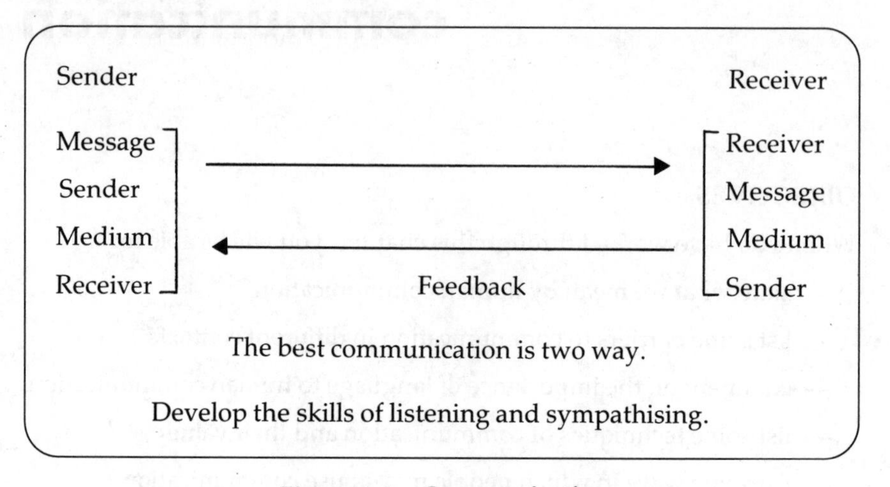

Figure 1.1 Communication

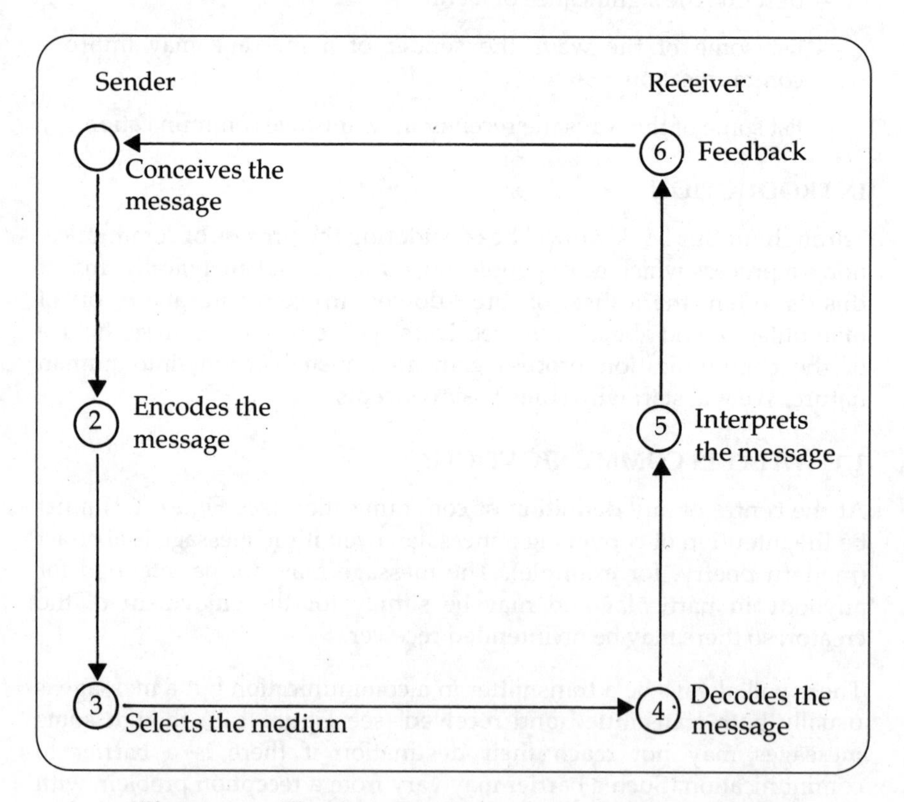

Figure 1.2 The theory and process of communication

A demonstration

Activity

(The tutor should ask one of the group to leave the room for a few minutes. The remaining students should copy a diagram something like this from the board.)

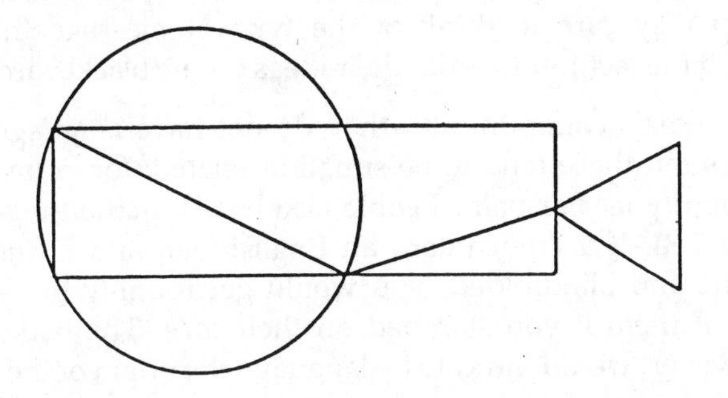

When copied, erase the diagram, cover the copies and invite the departed student to return. Instructions should then be given by the group (the lecturer hopes badly), to enable the returned student to re-draw the diagram. (Before the student re-enters the room, he/she should be requested to interpret the instructions as awkwardly as possible.) The person doing the drawing should not ask questions but should draw something absurdly wrong if, for example, no indication of size comes from the audience.

Discussion

The aim of this exercise is to show that a breakdown in the reception of a message will occur when the transmitter assumes an unreasonable amount of previous knowledge on the part of the receiver. This is a common mistake among teachers, though such examples will hopefully not be observed by the student of this course.

One can imagine the added confusion if the medium for this experiment had been the telephone. Additional problems would also have occurred if the receiver had not understood the terminology used. People working in particular environments (computer programming or engineering, for example), develop their own working terminology or restricted code to deal with specific events. The terms used may not be understood by those outside since, to the transmitter, they require an elaborated code to make understanding possible.

In all communications we must not take the receiver's understanding for granted.

Examples of breakdown in communication are given in the exercise at the end of section 1.4.

1.2 WHAT'S SO SPECIAL ABOUT COMMUNICATION?

What is so special about communication? Animals communicate with each other, often in elaborate ways. For example, a bee, discovering a plentiful supply of nectar several fields away from the hive, will return and give directions to its fellows by flying in a series of complex patterns in front of the hive. The other bees will then fly straight to the food source. Animal messages, however, tend to be limited in their purpose. (The group may care to think of the type of message that animals transmit and the lecturer to write their ideas on the blackboard.)

Although animals communicate, they do not have language. They do make noises but these tend to be situation-related: for example, a loud shriek to signify fear or pain. People also have situation-related noises (see Figure 1.3). If a Frenchman, an Englishman and a Russian were stood in line and blindfolded, you would get roughly the same noise from each of them if you stamped on their toes. The oaths that may follow, however, would indicate by language the origin of the sufferer.

Situation Context

- Role people find themselves in, eg stuck in a lift with your boss

Formality/Informality

- Degree of formality
- Effects on communication

Use of Space

- Positioning of furniture, eg being placed on a lower chair
- Physical proximity

Non-verbal Clues

- Facial expressions
- Gestures, hands, arms, nods
- Eye contact
- Unconscious signals

Figure 1.3 Other influences on communications

Jean Aitchison defines language as 'a patterned system of arbitrary sound symbols, whose characteristic features of displacement, cultural transmission, productivity and duality are rare or absent in animal communication' (*Teach yourself linguistics*, 2nd ed, Fontana, 1978). Some words are perhaps less random in their component sound than others:

for example the words buzz, fizz, pop and drip to some extent imitate that which they describe.

The debate on whether or not animals are capable of learning a language continues, concentrating in recent years on dolphin communications and the teaching of hand signals to apes. The miracle of human language acquisition remains a mystery. Why is it, for instance, that as infants we normally learn words and grammar at an incredible pace yet, when we have the know-how to analyse language in later years, we have such difficulty in learning enough French to buy things on holidays in France? The ability to communicate *is* special but it is often taken for granted and it is not always used to the greatest advantage (see Figure 1.4).

Sender	**Receiver**
Message wrongly conceived, vague, ambiguous. Affected by relationship of sender and receiver.	Feedback not given or wrongly interpreted by the sender
Message encoded in wrong language, tone inappropriate.	Message wrongly interpreted. Affected by relationship of receiver and sender. Ambiguous.
Wrong medium chosen: offence caused, time wasted, expense incurred, no written record, etc.	Receiver unable to comprehend sender's language. Vocabulary too difficult, specialist jargon used, etc.

Figure 1.4 Failure to communicate a message

1.3 HOW DO WE COMMUNICATE?

We communicate in a number of ways (see Figure 1.5). Consider which medium is most appropriate (look at the example shown in Figure 1.6 and the options shown in Figure 1.7). Most of the methods illustrated employ either the use of spoken language or written symbols that

The decision to send the message
- The result of an impulse
- Thought process
- Some external stimulus

Appropriate language chosen
- Written
- Oral
- Picture
- Non-verbal communication (unconscious signals)

Appropriate medium selected
- Letter
- Memo
- Phone call
- Meeting
- Interview

Signal passed to receiver
- Nod
- Eye contact
- Written or spoken reply

Interpretation
- Interpret the underlying meanings
- Explicit meanings in words chosen
- Particularly with non-verbal clues and intonation

Language used
- The language is decoded from knowledge of vocabulary used

Figure 1.5 Ways of communicating

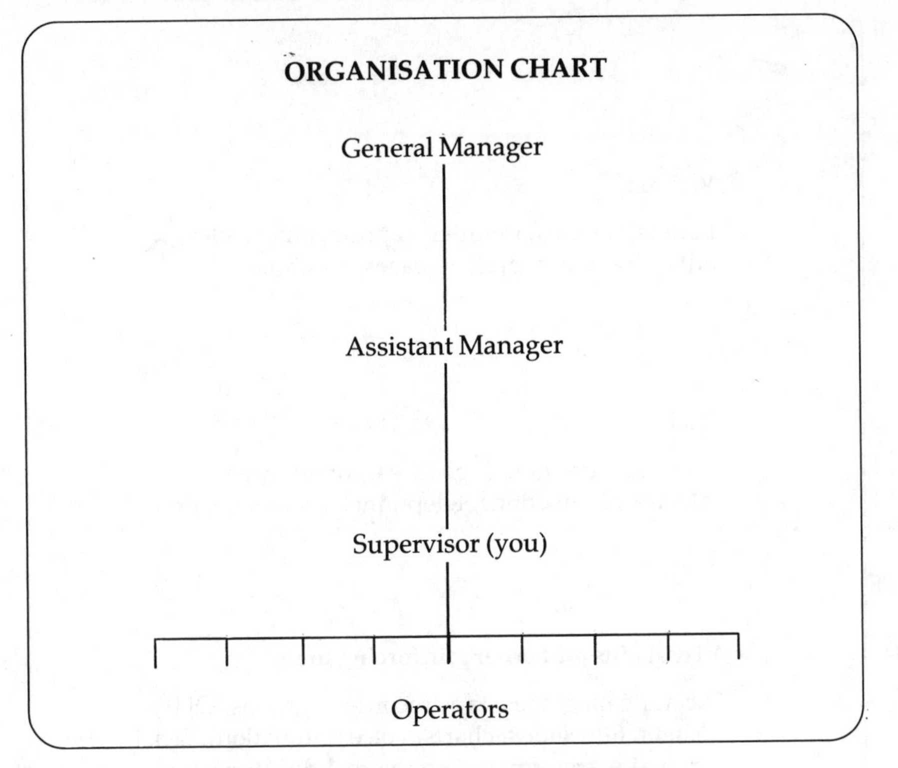

Figure 1.6 Exercise in communication

represent the speech sounds. Some of the messages make no use of language at all: we call this non-verbal communication. The road sign for falling rocks, for instance, is universal: it is likely to be understood by all nationalities, as are most road signs.

You are the supervisor of a small section of twenty people. The firm you work for has been experiencing problems, as it has recently lost an order from its main supplier. As a consequence, it has been suggested that your section be put on short-time working, (3 days a week) for a temporary period. The alternative is selective redundancies.

It is your responsibility to inform your section of the decision to implement a shorter working week.

1 What communication medium would you choose?

2 Why did you choose it?

Discuss the relative advantages and disadvantages of the other media available.

- **Written**

  Letters, memos, minutes, reports, notes, telex, advertisements, press releases, facsimile

- **Oral**

  Conversation, talks, speeches, conferences, interviews, meetings, telephone, intercom, video

- **Visual aids and other reinforcing tools**

  Dictating machines, tape recorders, graphs, OHPs, posters, film slides, charts, voice (intonation), facial expression (reinforcing non-verbal clues), posture

Figure 1.7 Media of communication

Non-verbal communication such as the use of gestures or mannerisms is often referred to as body language. The study of this aspect of non-verbal communication (NVC) has gained in popularity, due partly to the work of Desmond Morris. We all transmit messages non-verbally. What makes NVC particularly worthy of study is that we are not usually consciously aware of the messages. (The couple holding hands, on the other hand, is a communication of significance which both we and the couple are likely to consciously notice. Holding hands has acutely intense significance for the first few times a couple accept each other enough to hold hands, though it may become increasingly casual as the relationship develops. The message has clear significance to would-be suitors.)

Less understood are the unconscious signals of selling, job interviews, status and authority. The salesman who is aware of the importance of eye contact is more likely to sell. An interviewing panel will be influenced by a candidate's non-verbal communication as much as by spoken responses. Consider the seating in the boss's office – does the desk serve as a barrier? When seated, is the boss at a higher level than you are? Are you sitting directly opposite each other; if not, who has to look sideways? – all these factors can offer the opportunity for a superior to assert his or her authority without saying a word.

In addition to the deliberate verbal communication then, a second non-verbal level operates at which we are usually less aware. This second level of communication may account for what is sometimes called 'intuition': the ability to sense, for example, that a speaker's messages are suspect. We can see therefore that there are many different methods of communication, with various advantages and disadvantages (see Figures 1.8, 1.9 and 1.10).

WRITTEN COMMUNICATION

- Letters
- Reports
- Memos

ADVANTAGES	DISADVANTAGES
• Provides written record	• Takes time
• Evidence of despatch and receipt	• Can be expensive
• Can relay complex ideas	• More formal and impersonal
• Provides analysis, evaluation, summary	• Problems with interpretation
• Can be duplicated	• Feedback not instantaneous
• Can confirm, interpret, clarify oral communication	• Difficult to modify once sent
	• Exchange of views not immediately possible

Figure 1.8 Written communication

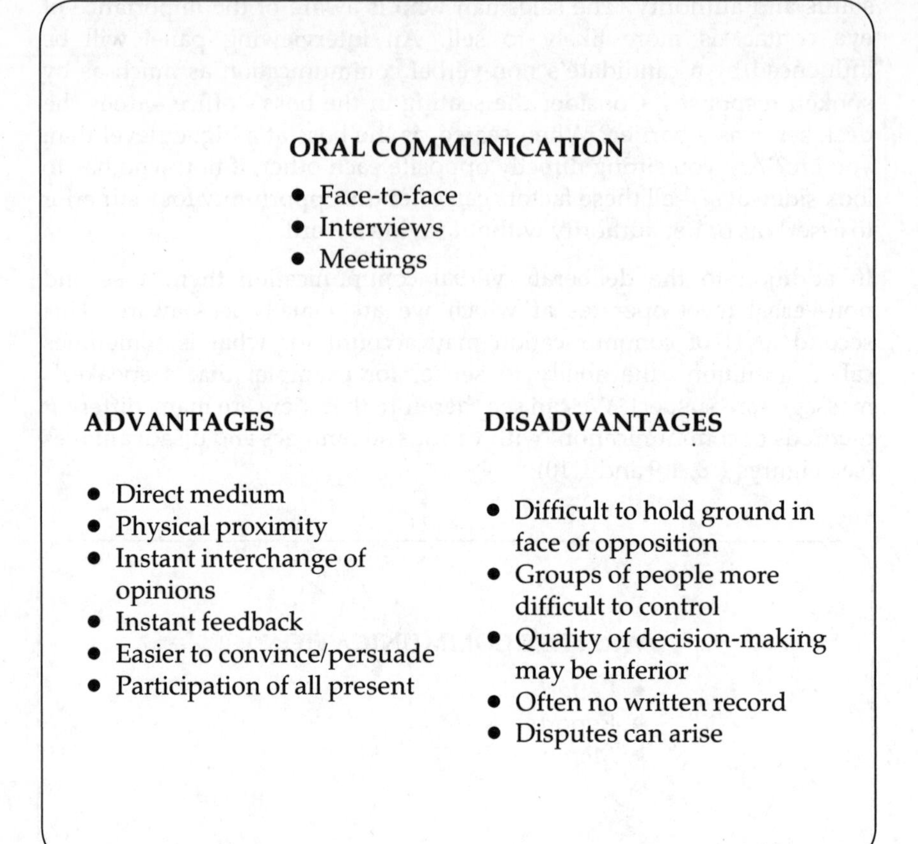

ORAL COMMUNICATION
• Face-to-face
• Interviews
• Meetings
ADVANTAGES
• Direct medium
• Physical proximity
• Instant interchange of opinions
• Instant feedback
• Easier to convince/persuade
• Participation of all present
DISADVANTAGES
• Difficult to hold ground in face of opposition
• Groups of people more difficult to control
• Quality of decision-making may be inferior
• Often no written record
• Disputes can arise

Figure 1.9 Oral communication

1.4 PEOPLE AND COMMUNICATION

Under normal circumstances, communication skills are available for us all to use. Expert communicators can use their skills to great effect, as one can witness with politicians and television presenters. Communication is also subject to abuse. A look at wartime propaganda shows how information can be transmitted in certain ways to achieve a particular effect. Even in current times, a comparison of newspaper articles covering the same news items will often reveal that some facts are being selected and interpreted for a particular purpose: perhaps to protect the ruling political power, to sensationalise scandalous aspects or to manipulate public opinion to a particular way of thinking. Analysis of newspaper reports prior to general elections is particularly fruitful in highlighting this aspect of communication.

Hopefully the link between people and communication is becoming apparent. It is not only the item of information or message that influences people, but the way in which the transmitter chooses to

NON-VERBAL COMMUNICATION

- Visual
- Charts, diagrams
- Unconscious signals

ADVANTAGES	DISADVANTAGES
• Reinforces oral communication • Added visual stimuli • Simplifies written and spoken word • Quantifies ideas in number form • Provides simulations of situations	• Difficulties in interpretation without written or spoken word • Skills in comprehension and interpretation a prerequisite • Can be expensive

Figure 1.10 Non-verbal communication

broadcast the message: from the selection of words to the way that they are presented. This course book recognises this link and aims not only to develop your communication skills but also to make you more aware of the communication process and its effect on others.

ACTIVITY

Describe someone who has left the room.

The group must try collectively to produce a written description of the missing person: height, weight, colour of eyes, hair colour and style, clothes, personal effects, etc. When finished, invite the person back into the room and compare your written description with the 'real thing'.

NOW TRY THESE . . .

1. Conceiving a message wrongly

A passenger is travelling by bus; it leaves bay 9 at 10.55 am. It is 10.55 and a bus is standing at bay 9. The passenger dashes there and asks 'Is this bay 9?' Another passenger answers 'yes'. The passenger jumps on the bus just as it leaves the station. Unfortunately it is the wrong bus. It is the one for a different destination which is late and also leaves from bay 9.

Explain what has gone wrong and where the breakdown fits into the 'circle' describing communication theory. (Include the second passenger's response.)

2. Ways of interpreting messages

a) A manager says to his junior 'You look tired'. How many ways could the message be interpreted by the junior?

b) Point out all the influences which could affect these interpretations.

3. Interpersonal skills

1. Your company has introduced vending machines and has withdrawn the trolley service which used to dispense refreshments to all the office staff. The machines have been giving trouble lately and suppliers say a lot of it is caused through ill-treatment by staff, who have been seen banging the machines in order to get their drinks.

One coffee break, David Dobbs, a youngish clerk with a reputation for a short temper, but regarded by most as a good worker, is seen by you throwing a half-full cup of coffee at the machine and kicking it violently with his right foot. As David's supervisor, you ask him to stop and to get a cloth to clean up the mess. He then turns to you and says 'I'm fed up, and if that's all the service I can get for my money you can clean the machine yourself'. With that he gathers up his things and storms out of the office.

Next day, he returns to work and carries on working as though nothing has happened.

As David's supervisor,

1. a) Suggest several different possible approaches that are available to you to deal with this incident.

   b) Describe in detail how you think you should conduct yourself in an interview with David.

2. a) Describe in detail, four major causes of communication breakdown at an interpersonal level.

   b) Describe, in detail, ways in which each of them can be avoided.

1.5 TECHNIQUES FOR IMPROVED COMMUNICATION

Feedback

An engineering term, 'feedback' refers to the ability of certain complex machines to check on their own performance and correct it if necessary. This principle is of prime importance in human communication. We must constantly be alert for clues to whether or not we are being understood (facial expression, head nods, etc).

The importance of feedback is illustrated by a simple exercise. Two students are seated back-to-back with a table in front of each of them. Identical sets of children's building blocks are placed on the tables. One of the students proceeds to build any structure he chooses, using all the blocks, and at the same time instructs the other student to build an identical structure. The receiver is forbidden to respond in any way. The absence of feedback makes the task, in most cases, impossible, as false perceptions creep in and minor errors go uncorrected and become magnified. Additionally, the exercise makes the point that communication gains in speed as more and more feedback is permitted.

Using a number of communication channels

Observation

In a face-to-face situation we can observe the other person and judge his responses by his 'total behavioural set', ie changes of facial expression and more subtle body movements that communicate anger, disbelief, impatience, etc. Tone of voice is equally informative, for example as a measurement of enthusiasm.

Listening with the 'third ear'

There is a hidden content in most communication which can only be inferred by the listener (*latent* content, versus *manifest* content). The listener should try to go beyond the logical verbal meaning where there is evidence that emotion is involved, bearing in mind the need to keep imagination in check.

Speaking patterns

It is important to be aware of the difference in speaking patterns. Some people speak with drawn-out pauses between thoughts or sentences, and if they are interrupted they fail to reveal all their original ideas. Failure to adjust and to synchronise to the speech patterns of others, as well as causing ideas to be lost, can result in long silent periods which can cause discomfort.

The merits of face-to-face communication

- — Ease, through frequency of use of voice rather than written medium.
- — Immediacy of feedback.
- — More credibility is given to what we hear someone say rather than to words attributed to them in print.

However, it is important to note that written communication allows both for more permanency and for easier assimilation of complex material. In the case of the need to communicate with a larger number of people, written communication is also administratively more convenient.

Sensitivity to the world of the receiver

We need to predict the impact of what we say and do, tailoring our message to fit the receiver's vocabulary, emotional state, interests and values; in short we need to empathise.

Awareness of symbolic meaning

We must try and be aware of the symbolic meaning of what we say and write and be prepared to revise our statements if they evoke unfavourable reactions, however irrational they may appear to us.

The timing of messages

Consider the following example: Management announces that a foreman, Green, is to retire and will be replaced in a few months by Williams, at present employed in another department. One of the employees spreads a rumour that Williams is a tyrant who favours 'crawlers'. Before Williams takes up the new post, a petition is sent to Management asking for a different foreman to be assigned. When Williams finally takes up his new post, everything he says and does is fitted to the picture already built up; even harmless statements are interpreted as threats and every action scrutinised for favouritism! What lessons are to be learned from this situation?

Introducing redundancy

When giving a direct order or transmitting technical information we should make sure that the message includes a certain element of redundancy. Then, if any word or phrase is misunderstood, there will be other elements of the message which will carry the point. Familiarity can also lead to communication breakdown; we tend to ignore many of the messages which we receive simply because they sound familiar. The problem, in short, is to balance the need for redundancy to support words and phrases of crucial importance and the need to achieve a pattern which has originality and avoids repetition of clichés.

This techniques section can be summed up as:

Efforts to communicate	Feedback Many channels Face-to-face communication Sensitivity to receiver Symbolic meanings Timing of messages Redundancy	Clear message

A REMINDER: USING THE COMMUNICATION PROCESS EFFECTIVELY

Remember these ways to improve communication:

As the sender

- When composing a message decide what action or response you want.
- Choose the language or combination of written/spoken/non-verbal communication most suitable for the type of communication.
- Take time to structure your ideas logically.
- Select the medium which is most likely to achieve your aim.
- Put yourself in the receiver's position. Will he/she understand the words chosen? What is the context? What seems to be his/her emotional state?
- Take care that the message cannot be misunderstood. Avoid being vague or ambiguous.
- Check for feedback. Decide if you need to answer. Look for an indication of attitude.

As the receiver

- Give the message your whole attention.
- Check that the medium suits your needs; tactfully give help if this is inappropriate.
- Ensure full comprehension. Check references and ask for explanations if necessary.
- Check that *you* understand correctly. Is there an underlying meaning or implication? Check the manner in which the message is communicated.
- Ensure you supply sufficient and appropriate feedback.

NOW TRY THESE...

1. You are the office clerk in a small company. As there are few office staff you have a variety of duties to perform. As well as general office tasks, you are responsible for opening the mail in the morning and forwarding it to its correct department. It is Monday morning and you find the items that follow (Figures 1.11 to 1.18) in your in-tray. It is your task to deal with them as efficiently as possible; to help you do this, follow the procedure given below:
   a) arrange the mail in order of priority;
   b) state what action you would take for each item;
   c) complete any written forms of communication necessary.
2. a) The Best Communication Is Two Way. Explain this sentence with an example.
   b) Explain the importance of 'Feedback' in effective communication.
3. a) What are the major causes of communication breakdown at an inter-personal level?
   b) How can these best be avoided?

Can you order some more coffee – we've run out!
Thanks

Dina

Dina

Figure 1.11 An informal note

VISION GRAPHICS

MEMORANDUM

To: Miss Lewis Date 2.3.92

From: Transport Dept. Reference TJ/RA

Subject:

Ring Eastleigh 2231 to book Mr. Richards' car for a 12,000-mile service, today if possible.

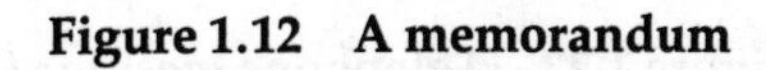

Figure 1.12 A memorandum

MESSAGE FORM

Time of call 5 pm........................... Date 27.2.92..........................
Name of caller Sue Lewis..
Name and address of firm
....
....
....
Tel. no 456544 Ext. no...
Receiver of call Jenny Lewis...

MESSAGE:

Your sister, Sue, phoned late Friday afternoon. She has no idea what to buy your parents for their silver wedding anniversary. Have you any suggestions?

Can you ring her when you have a spare moment?

Taken by Sara Jones...

Figure 1.13 Telephone message (1)

VISION GRAPHICS

MEMORANDUM

To: All Staff Date 27.2.92

From: Secretary of Staff Club Reference:

Subject:

We must know as soon as possible, how many staff want to come on the trip to London next Saturday. Otherwise it may have to be cancelled.

Figure 1.14 A staff circular

12 Oak Road
Kings Park
Hoxley
HK29 4QP

27.2.92

The Personnel Manager
Vision Graphics
2 Low Street
Hoxley
HL19 4QZ

Dear Sir or Madam,

My father used to work for your company until he retired two years ago. I have recently been made redundant by Jones & Co. Ltd. I am a skilled printer and would welcome the opportunity to work for you, if there should happen to be any vacancies.

Your faithfully,

Paul Green

Paul Green

Figure 1.15 Incoming letter (1)

VISION GRAPHICS

MEMORANDUM

To: Miss Lewis | Date 2.3.92

From: Peter Richards, Manager | Reference SH/PR

Subject: Taxi

Please order me a taxi for 9.30 am, to take me to a meeting at Thomas and Sons Ltd., High Street.

Figure 1.16 A sample memorandum

12 Long Lane
Cofton
Birmingham
B30 2ES

26th February 1992

Vision Graphics
2 Low Street
Hoxley
HL19 4QZ

Dear Sir or Madam,
I asked for a quotation for a cover design for our local magazine three weeks ago. As yet I have heard nothing from you. I would greatly appreciate a reply as soon as possible.

Yours faithfully,

E. Roberts

E. Roberts

Figure 1.17 Incoming letter (2)

MESSAGE FORM

Time of call 9 am .... Date 2.3.92

Name of caller Tony Lyons – Sales Manager ....

Name and address of firm

....

....

....

Tel. no .... Ext. no 35

Receiver of call Jenny Lewis ....

MESSAGE:

Can you book a 1st class seat on a train to London tomorrow morning at about 9 am for Tony.

Let him know the departure time as soon as possible.

Taken by Sarah Jones ....

Figure 1.18 Telephone message (2)

2 Study skills

OBJECTIVES

When you have worked through this chapter, you will be able to:

— explain the SQ3R approach to reading lengthy material

— list ways to improve the efficiency of reading

— list ways to improve the speed of reading

— explain the importance of *skim reading*

— state the nature of, and compare, linear and patterned note taking

— outline the use of a library's author and subject catalogues and reference section.

INTRODUCTION

Reading is a skill we all take very much for granted. It has probably not occurred to you that you can teach yourself to read *better* and *faster*. This chapter aims to point you in this direction and by the time you have worked through the exercises you should be a better and faster reader than you were before. Another important skill, in study and elsewhere, is making good notes. We explore that here also.

2.1 HOW TO IMPROVE YOUR READING

One very useful approach to studying any written material (a handout, a book or an article), is known as the SQ3R approach, ie Survey, Question, Read, Recall, Review, (see Figure 2.1). These five steps are briefly explained below:

— *Survey* the material first, to get some idea of what parts (if any) you will need to study in detail. To help you in this task, scan the table of contents; if the book has a full description of the contents of chapters this is often a useful guide. The Preface or Introduction may also be useful in helping you find out quickly what the book is about. If a particular chapter looks of interest note it but don't read it yet. First look to see if there is a summary – perhaps at the end; check headings to sections and any emphasised sections.

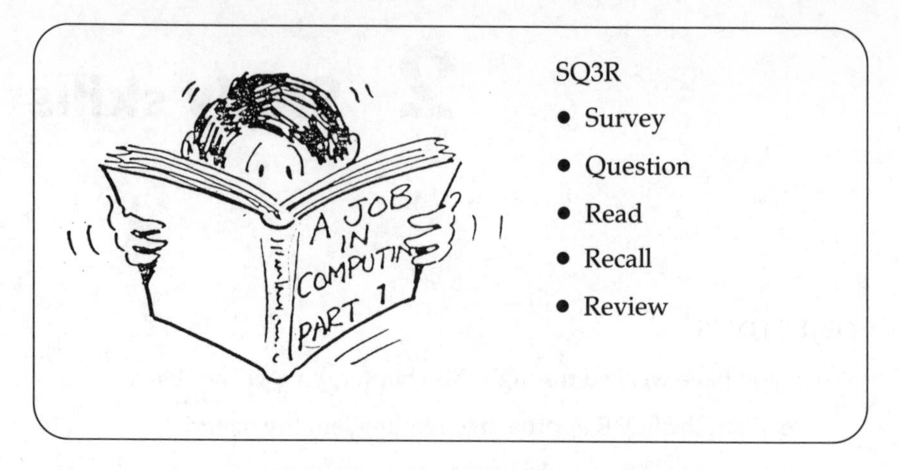

Figure 2.1 How to improve your reading

— Think up *questions* that will give purpose to your study and allow you to read with anticipation (eg 'Why does the author divide up his material in this way?', 'What are the main themes: are these useful to me?').

— *Read* the material (preferably two or three times quite fast rather than once slowly).

— Stop after each section of material to *recall* what you have read and make brief notes of the main ideas and important details. Is the section of key importance to you?

— *Review* what you have read (to test the accuracy of your notes) by quickly running through the four previous steps again.

During the 'Read' stage of SQ3R:

— Pick out the main idea in each paragraph – often this will be contained in the first or last sentence.

— Look for important details, eg proofs, examples, supports for main idea.

— Study the author's diagrams and illustrations – they make clear what the text does not.

— Be sceptical. Don't take the author's word on trust; look for him to justify every statement he makes. (If he doesn't and the point is an important one, check with another book or fellow student and later with your lecturer.)

— Don't be afraid to skip paragraphs and whole sections if you can see that they are not relevant to your purpose. There's no law that says you've got to read every page of a book.

— If, after chewing over a particular section for some time, you still find it difficult to understand, take a break. Try to discuss the difficulty with other students or with a lecturer or find another author's treatment of the topic; then come back and read the passage again – two or three times if necessary.

HOW TO READ FASTER

Being able to read faster (see Figure 2.2) will enable you to use the ideas on how to read better (above), to get the best possible overall results. Most students spend a great deal of time working on books and other printed materials. They would be able to use this time more effectively if they could read faster. And the truth is that most people could read at least as fast again as their normal speed, and still understand just as well. Slow readers tend to read one word at a time, often mouthing the words as they do so, and to take frequent glances back at words they have already seen. Some read so slowly that by the time they have got to the end of a paragraph, or even a sentence, they may have forgotten how it began. Here are five ways you can start helping yourself to read faster:

— Have your eyes tested – many people turn out to need reading glasses for continuous study.

— Make sure you don't mouth words or say them aloud as you read.

— Try to take in 'thought-units' (two or three words at a time) so that your eye stops only three or four times in a line of print instead of at every word.

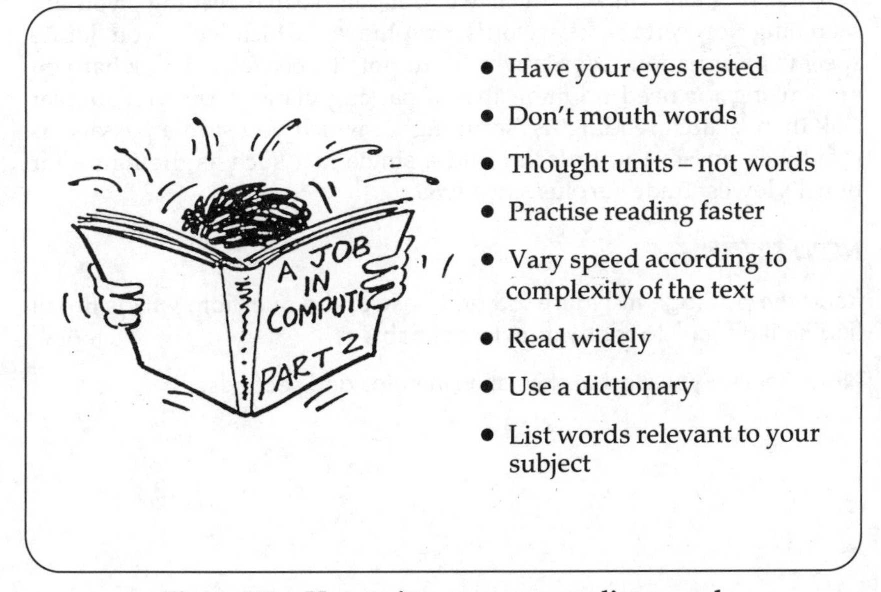

A JOB IN COMPUTI
PART 2
• Have your eyes tested
• Don't mouth words
• Thought units – not words
• Practise reading faster
• Vary speed according to complexity of the text
• Read widely
• Use a dictionary
• List words relevant to your subject

Figure 2.2 How to increase your reading speed

— Practise reading faster (force yourself) by, for example:

a) timing your reading of magazine articles of known length – and test your recall of the contents;

b) reading all your study material faster, even if you have to read it more than once.

The aim of the above exercises is to be able to vary your reading speed according to the complexity of the material and the purpose for which you are reading it. If you are simply trying to get the overall gist of a piece of narrative, you should be able to read two or three times as fast as when you are trying to unravel the detailed development of a complex argument. But even when the material is particularly difficult, you may benefit from scanning through it quickly first before you get down to reading it more intensively. Don't expect every piece of text you look at to yield its full meaning immediately.

Build up your vocabulary by the following methods:

— Read widely.

— Use a dictionary whenever new words crop up in your reading; note new words.

— Make a list of the meanings of words commonly used in your subjects; this vocabulary-broadening activity should be separate from your practice at reading faster.

Now read the passage given in Exercise 1. Carefully note the time, in minutes and seconds, at which you start reading and the time at which you finish. In this task, which we will call 'search reading', you are searching for certain key words or phrases which help you locate specific information. Words which are not closely related to what you are looking for need no more than a passing glance. An even simpler task than 'search reading' is 'scanning' in which you scan a passage as rapidly as possible in order to find a single fact such as the figure for Brazil's lowest trade surplus since 1983.

NOW TRY THIS...

Read the passage in Figure 2.3 and answer the question: why is Brazil finding it difficult to repay its external debt?

Note the time you start and finish in minutes and seconds.

Fears rise over Brazil debts

BY IVO DAWNAY AND ALEXANDER NICOLL

CONCERN WAS mounting last night that the fall in Brazil's foreign trade surplus would shortly force it to delay repayments on its $109bn (£71.43bn) external debt.

There was no official confirmation of rumours that the Brazilian Government was about to suspend payments, but foreign bankers are conscious of the gravity of the situation. They expect a delay of some kind, though not necessarily an official moratorium.

The severity of Brazil's crisis was underlined by Mr Paul Volcker, chairman of the US Federal Reserve Board, who told a congressional committee that the country was in a 'grave economic crisis.'

The Fed chairman also issued an urgent warning about the outlook for the Third World debt problems.

Describing the strategy for tackling the debt problem, the so-called 'Baker plan' was 'bogged down' by the failure of complete bank financings for a number of heavily indebted nations. Mr Volcker said: 'This is threatening the whole process.'

Mr Volcker said confidence had been lost in Brazil. In spite of firm, constructive steps that had made the economy competitive for a while, high inflation had returned and the trade position had deteriorated. These factors could make it difficult to raise money from commercial banks.

Brazil's ambassador to the US, Mr Marcilio Marques Moreira, was reported to have returned to Washington after consultations with President Jose Sarney and other top officials. He was expected to spell out to the US the seriousness of Brazil's shortage of funds.

One Brazilian official quoted by Reuters said: 'We are going to have to warn creditors that we cannot pay more than we can afford.'

Rumours of a debt move and of impending economic measures pushed the dollar sharply higher on Brazil's illegal black market. It rose as high as Cr 30 compared with official rates of about Cr 18.5. Gold prices also rose 10 per cent above the New York market price.

Foreign bankers believe a delay in payments could take the form of a centralisation of exchange controls, and that it would be accompanied by assurances that Brazil was taking the step out of necessity and not in defiance of its creditors.

Another option being mooted is a formal suspension of some repayments for a short period, perhaps three months. This would give Brazil a breathing space while it negotiated fresh arrangements with creditors.

The recent sharp deterioration in Brazil's payments position is expected to heighten pressure on the Government to relax its steadfast refusal to adopt a programme of economic adjustment under the unspices of the International Monetary Fund.

Brazil was counting on at least a $1bn monthly trade surplus to meet its payments, but in January the surplus was the lowest since 1983, dropping to a mere $129m from $701m a year ago.

Brazil's trade surplus began its downward fall last October, when it dropped to $210m. Since 1984, it had been averaging more than $1bn a month – enough to meet the interest payments.

Figure 2.3 Extract from *The Financial Times*

Skimming

So far we have looked at what might be called 'receptive reading', where you have little clear purpose beyond needing to obtain a good general understanding, and at 'search reading' and 'scanning', where your purpose is very clear. A question which remains is: how do you decide on your purpose until you have found out what an author has to say?
For this, and for other reasons, 'skimming' (see Figure 2.4) is a very useful skill. Skimming involves going rapidly through a text while making certain judgements, and remembering only certain things. It may be used:

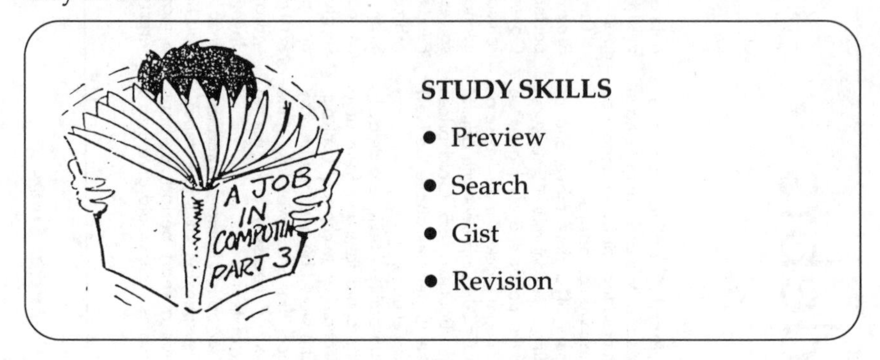

Figure 2.4 Skim reading

- — To decide, by previewing a text, whether to read it in total and if so why to read it (ie for what purpose).
- — To decide how to read it (eg whether to read carefully making detailed notes, or merely to use it for search reading in order to gain information on a certain topic).
- — To read it to obtain a rough idea of what the writer has to say (ie for the gist of his meaning).
- — To review something you have already read, for revision for an examination or to refresh your memory for some other purpose.

The important common factor in all these uses of skimming is that they involve selectivity on the part of the reader. Skimming is always done quickly: at a speed at least two and a half to three times that which you would use to read the passage if you were using receptive reading rather than skimming. One other use of skimming is, strange as it may seem, in tackling very difficult texts. It will sometimes be better to read text through quickly two or three times, without attempting full understanding of the more baffling points, until they become gradually clearer.

2.2 MAKING NOTES

Notes provide a brief written record of larger pieces of work, eg an article, a chapter in a book, a talk or a television programme. Making notes keeps your mind active as you read. It makes you think and concentrate – so you learn and remember better. Don't forget, however, that there may be alternatives to note-taking you may wish to use, eg underlining in a book.

The important things to remember in note-taking are:

— The main ideas and themes must be clear.

— Avoid detail and repetition.

— Your notes must mean something to *you* so wherever possible *use your own words*.

— Use a system which works for you.

How to make notes

Linear note-making

This is the traditional type of note-making which most of us are familiar with. Headings and sub-headings are used, with lettering, numbering and indentations used for sections and sub-sections. You will see that parts of this book are set out in this way.

Although you are probably already familiar with this form of note-making, try the exercises on page 33. You will find that linear notes can be useful for summarising existing information but may not be so useful for such things as trying to recall previously learned material or even generating new ideas round a topic.

Patterned note-making

Traditional linear notes look very neat but may not show adequately the relationships between the ideas and themes in the subject you are noting. You may therefore find that you need to approach note-making from a different angle. A useful alternative to linear notes is patterned notes which link together key ideas/concepts. The basic unit is a 'spray' of ideas, as shown on Figure 2.5.

Uses for patterned notes:

— for recalling things or for generating new ideas;

— for making your own notes from written or spoken material.

Tips for patterns:

— Use only *Key Words* – don't waste time on unnecessary words.

— All words should be *Printed* for ease of reading.

— Arrange the printed words *On* the *Lines* which link up the various parts of the pattern.

When you are using patterns for recall or creativity let your mind go free. You will be surprised at the speed with which you generate ideas.

Exercise in patterned note-making

Without pausing for further thought write down as much information as you can in the form of *Key Words on Lines* to form a pattern around a particular topic, eg the basic economical decisions which firms have to make in order to survive in the commercial world.

Problems

The difficulties you may have experienced are most likely to have been:

— organisation and order;

— sequence of ideas;

— importance of some ideas (priorities);

— beginning and ending.

Solutions

If you are using patterns for note-making from a book or lecture, it may be a good idea to use two pages of notes concurrently or to use an A4 page on its side, using one side for patterns, the other for linear detail or diagrams, etc.

EXERCISE

Using library and reference sources

Catalogues

Look up and write down the following in the Author catalogue:

— the titles of two books by a writer whose surname begins with A

— the name of two publications issued by the Department (or Ministry) of Education

— the names of published books by J D Salinger

Look up and write down the following in the Subject catalogue:

— the titles of two books with the classification numbers of 001.64 and 301.42

— the classification number of the subject Japanese Cookery

Periodicals

Find out which periodicals relevant to Business Studies are taken by the library.

Information sources

- List the information sources provided by the Quick Reference Section of your Central Library.
- List the titles of reference material which would be useful to a large exporting company.

General information

Provide answers to the following questions and list the source of your information. If possible provide more than one information source:

- Locate a suitable hotel in your nearest city for an overnight stay for a business man requiring conference facilities.
- The rate of exchange of the £ at 2.00 pm today.
- The currency of Greece and its rate of exchange in £ sterling and US dollars.

Reference books

Provide answers to the following questions and name your reference source:

- Times of flights from the capital to New York arriving before 5.30 pm local times (Mon to Fri).
- Can you fly from Tunis airport to Bombay?
- What is the European Development Fund?
- How many years service do female employees have to accumulate to be eligible for maternity leave and pay?
- What categories of tax do companies pay on their profits?
- What was the national value of exports in 1990?
- What is the current bank rate?
- Give the name and address of a company that manufactures protective clothing.
- What law governs fire safety in work places?
- What was the total in £ sterling of French imports to the UK in 1980?
- What was the gross profit of the country's vehicles industry in 1988?
- Give the name and address of a company that sells vending machines.
- What was the total national number of unemployed in 1990?
- What is the capital of Yugoslavia and name its government leaders.

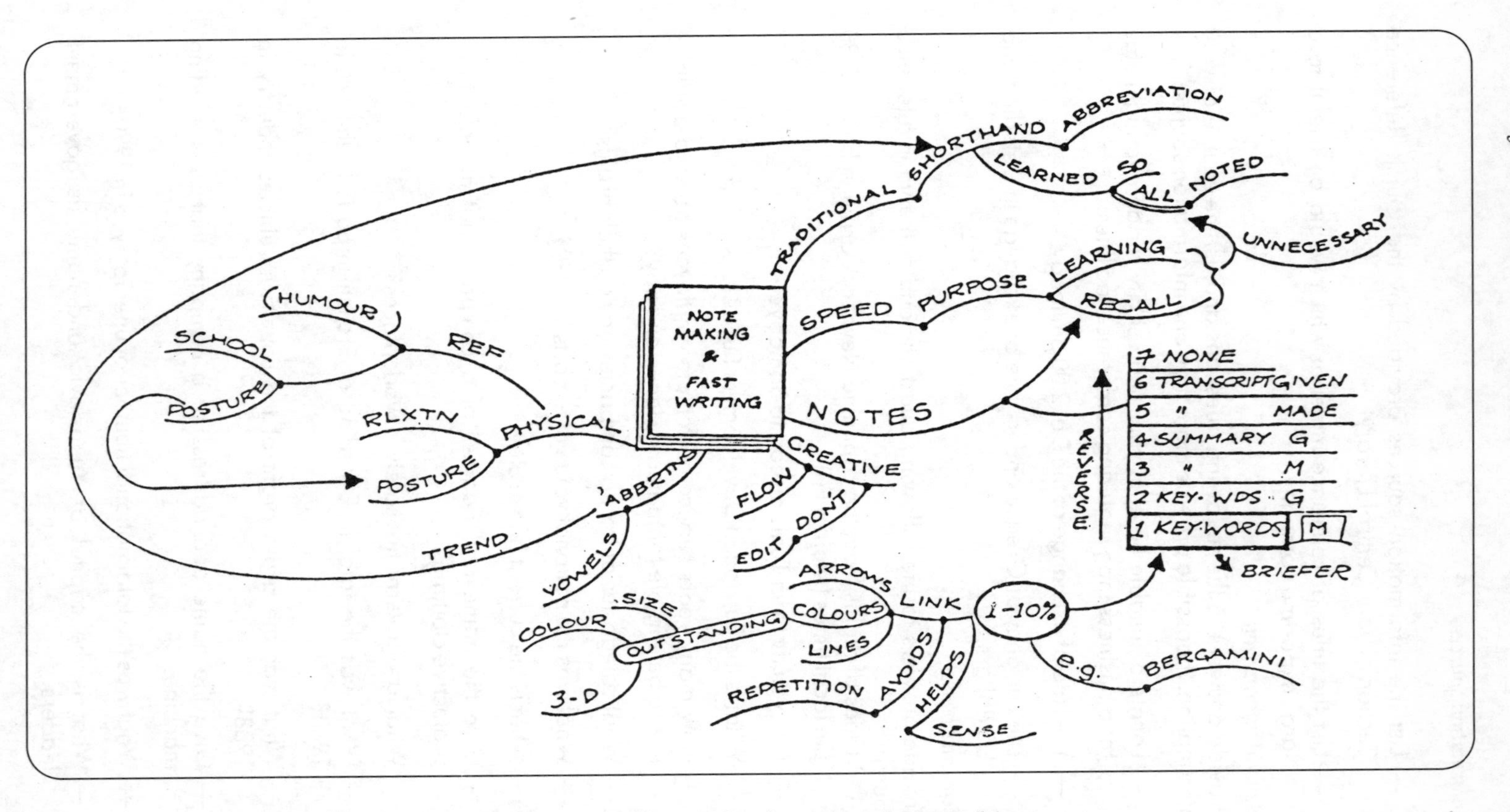

Figure 2.5 An example of patterned note-taking

NOW TRY THESE...

1. Rewrite in linear narrative form the weather conditions in this area of the West Midlands for today through until tomorrow afternoon (Figure 2.6). Make a comparison between these temperatures and those in Europe over the same period.

	This Evening	Tonight	Tomorrow morning	Tomorrow afternoon
Weather	Dry	Dry	Dry	Dry
State of sky	Bright	Broken	Bright	Bright
Temperature	15(59F)	10C(45F)	13C(59F)	15C(59F)
Wind	Light SSW	Light S	Mod S	Mod SW
Remarks	Isolated showers possible.			
Outlook for the following day: Dry, sunny spells.				

Birmingham Airport Met Office reading for the 24 hours to 0900 hours today:-

Maximum temperature: 20.7C(69.3F).

Night minimum temperature: 6.8C(44.2F).

Sunshine: 11.2 hours.

Rainfall: Nil.

Humidity: 0600 hours 97%, 1200 hours 64%, 1800 hours 49%

Barometer: corrected to sea level (0900 hrs), 1020.7 mb (30.14 ins).

Wind: SE, 8 mph.

Sea passages: Channel, North Sea: Slight.
Irish Sea: Moderate.

SUN AND MOON

Sun rises 6.02, sets 8.10. Moon rises 1.14 am, sets 7.52 am.

WEATHER ABROAD

Algiers: s, 20C(68F); Amsterdam: s, 15C(59F); Athens: c, 17C(63F); Barcelona: s, 17C(63F); Berlin: s, 13C(55F); Copenhagen: c, 9C(48F); Dublin: s, 13C(55F); Florence: s, 19C(66F); Geneva: s, 17C(63F); Innsbruck: s, 18C(64F); Lisbon: c, 19C(66F); Majorca: s, 18C(64F); Malta: s, 17C(63F); Nice: s, 16C(61F); Oslo: f, 13C(55F); Paris: s, 21(70F); Stockholm: f, 9C(48F); Vienna: f,15C(59F).
Key: s, sunny; c, cloudy; f, fair.

Figure 2.6 Extract from the *Birmingham Evening Mail*

2. Reproduce the substance of the article below: 'Somalia famine as rains fail' (Figure 2.7), in note form, using not more than 125 words in all (the original is around 400 words in length). It is not necessary to avoid the wording of the original but you will obviously earn credit for the intelligent selection of material and the logical arrangement of your notes.

Somalia famine as rains fail

From Shyama Perera in Mogadishu
THE Somali Government is to declare a drought emergency after the failure of the spring rains for the second year in succession. Up to two million people could be affected.

Nomads living in the central region of the country have reported many cattle dead or dying, and there has been an influx of displaced persons and livestock to neighbouring towns.

About 54 people, mainly children, are known to have died already from drought-related diseases, but it is thought the real figure is over 300. The Ministry of the Interior said yesterday that if the rains had not come by the end of this week, they would declare the central region an emergency area. This would allow donors to release reserve funds to finance food and water stocks.

Surrounding areas, such as the river town of Giohar, have had some rain, and water levels are high. But there is little or no grazing and the survival rate of nomadic livestock in the area is low because they are often too weak to move and fall victim to sleeping sickness carried by the tsetse fly.

Conditions around the central region of Galgadud are said to be critical. Mr Cadbi Arden Noor, permanent secretary at the Ministry of the Interior, said adequate water supplies were being trucked to the worst areas and Oxfam had installed hand-pumps at bore holes for nomads who could not afford trucked supplies. However, these are only stalling tactics and in one of the hardest hit areas, Dusa Mareb, food supplies ran out 20 days ago.

The roads are already strewn with the carcases of dead animals and the air is filled with the stench of rotting flesh. In Somalia, with its 65 per cent nomadic population, livestock is the equivalent of currency.

Oxfam's Somalia director, Mr Steve Cavell, said yesterday that upwards of 100,000 people could be left destitute through loss of livestock.

Even if the rains break through in the next week, it will do little to ease the situation and will cause widespread disease among those with weakened resistance as a result of malnutrition and dehydration.

Nomad migration patterns throughout the country indicate this crisis could be worse than the crippling drought of 1975.

Figure 2.7 Excerpt from *The Guardian*

3. Read the following extract adapted from *Quality Circles in Action* by M. Robson and answer the questions below.

"Though Quality Circles first developed in Japan during the late 1950s and early 1960s, the approach is based on Western theories of management, notably Douglas McGregor's Theory Y..."

"Firstly Quality Circles is an approach which allows people to become more involved, but puts no pressure on them to do so, in other words the approach is entirely voluntary at all levels of the organisation..."

"Secondly people who join in are encouraged to solve their own job-related problems... "

"Thirdly members solve their problems in an organised way, in other words they are given training in the skills of systematic problem solving and of working together effectively in a group..."

"A Quality Circle consists of a group of 4 to 10 volunteers who work for the same first-line supervisor and who meet regularly to identify, analyse and solve work problems..."

"... the group does not need to consist of the entire workforce from that section": only those that volunteer.

"... the group meet regularly once a week, for an hour and in paid time ..."

"... the groups at their meetings do not stop at the identification of problems for passing on to management, for solution, they utilise the training they receive to analyse and solve them and then present their own findings to management..."

"... there are 3 main possible goals: staff involvement, people development and the generation of tangible benefits..." for the organisation and people in it.

a) Outline in detail in your own words **four** possible benefits for the company of introducing Quality Circles.

b) Consider and explain in detail **five** problems the company might encounter in establishing and operating Quality Circles.

4. Read carefully the following extracts from the Employer's Guide to Pay as You Earn:

The Pay As You Earn method of deducting income tax from salaries and wages applies to all income from offices held (except in a few isolated types of case for which the employers concerned will be given special instructions). Thus Pay As You Earn applies not only to wages and salaries but also to annual payments, bonuses, commissions, directors' fees, pensions, and any other income or emoluments.

Under Pay As You Earn the amount of tax which the employer has to deduct depends on the employee's total gross pay since the beginning of the income tax year.

Where an employer has an arrangement under which meal vouchers are issued to his employees, the value of the vouchers issued to an employee is not regarded as part of his taxable income provided the following conditions are satisfied:

(1) the vouchers are non-transferable and used for meals only;

(2) where any restriction is placed on their issue to employees they are available to the lower paid staff;

(3) the value of the vouchers issued to an employee does not exceed $1 for each full working day.

Where the condition (3) is not satisfied the value in excess of 15 cents a day is regarded as taxable income and is to be shown in a return at the end of the tax year.

(a) What difference is there between 'wages' and 'salaries'?
Can you suggest any reasons why an employer or employee might have a preference for using one of these terms instead of the other?

(b) What do you understand by the term 'offices held'?

(c) What, broadly speaking, is the difference between 'bonus' and 'commission'?

(d) A company decides to issue meal vouchers to its senior staff only. Comment on the tax position.

(e) What is 'gross pay'? When the tax has been deducted and the employee receives his pay, suggest an expression to replace 'gross pay'.

(f) What is a 'return'.

(g) Your employer plans to issue meal vouchers worth $1.50 a day to all his staff. Prepare a short explanatory statement which can be printed on a slip of paper to be inserted into each employee's pay packet together with his weekly supply of vouchers. Use the relevant material from the passage and make your answer roughly 50-60 words in length.

5. Read the following extract and answer the questions below:

THE EFFECTS OF AUTHORITY AND RESPONSIBILITY

The Effect of Authority

The effects on communication of the holding of a position of authority or responsibility are often overlooked, though they can be very significant. The holding of a post carrying authority can easily lead a communicator to take the attitude that his word is law, and that his instructions and opinions should be accepted without question. Nowadays this is not necessarily the case. The recipients of a communication will question it, seek explanations, or even try to *amend* it with their own ideas. The authority held by the originator does not command automatic acceptance.

Nevertheless, authority does add weight to a communication, and the wise communicator in this position uses this to add force to his message whilst at the same time he takes into account the likely reaction that may result. He will probably find it necessary, therefore, to *temper his authority* with explanations in order that he may gain the response he requires.

The Effect of Responsibility

Whilst the holding of authority gives rise to considerations of acceptance, the holding of responsibility gives rise to considerations of consequence. The fact that the communicator will be held responsible for the outcome of his communication should make him use more caution than he would if he were not be held accountable for the consequences of his communication. Perhaps the most public example of the way responsibility affects attitude can be seen in Parliament. The party in power talks and acts with much more caution than it did when in opposition: in the latter case it knew quite well it could not be held *accountable* for its ideas or its utterances. Responsibility usually, therefore, causes more care and consideration to be given to the possible consequences of words and actions than if there were no responsibility, and this in turn results in more *restrained* and carefully worded communications. The use and abuse of authority and of responsibility in communication have a considerable effect on staff receptiveness and hence on the effectiveness of communication within an organisation, particularly vertically downwards.

a) Give the meaning of the following 3 words as they are used in the passage:

amend
accountable
restrained

b) Give the meaning of the following phrase as it is used in the passage:

temper his authority

c) What recent change in attitude towards authority is outlined in the passage?

d) Summarise the political analogy used in the passage.

6. Read the following passage and answer the questions below:

The Flexible Time-Clock

Flexible working hours is a system which, by putting an end to the nine to five working day myth, brings a more human touch to the working situation, without forcing anybody into another straitjacket, It does not demand, either, that the individual, who is set in his or her ways, should change their habits. With flexible working hours, the working day is split into three sections – one when everyone must be present (the core time) and two at either end of the day (the flexible bands) when everyone can come and go as they please.

It is now estimated that there are well over 2,000 applications of the system. It has been adopted in administrative organisations, retailing, insurance companies, and head offices, as well as in local and central government.

In the system core times are set to coincide with the daily peak demands on the organisation – in an office from 10am until 4pm and flexible bands are added during which employees can be present or not at their will. In the office situation, these might well be between 8am and 10am and 4pm and 6.30pm. The main restrictions, apart from presence during the core time, is that over a given settlement period, which can be a week or a fortnight, but more usually a month, have contracted, ie if the contracted time is seven hours per day, they have to be present in total for 140 hours in a month of 20 working days. There are refinements. Many companies have added an additional flexible band to cover the lunch break. Employees can take up to 1.5 hours, but they must observe a minimum of half-an-hour. Most companies which have implemented this system allow a further concession; the possibility of a debit or credit carry forward of up to ten hours. Debit/credit hours should be made up, or taken, during the flexible bands of the following settlement period; but some companies allow a half-day per month off in core time against accumulated credit hours.

It is not all 'blue skies' however. But nor has the old adage that if you give a man enough rope he will hang himself proved true, either. In a typical firm, employees are almost always in credit to the tune of, on average, approximately four hours per employee. Also there are other advantages to the company.

Out of a total of thirty companies replying, to a questionnaire, improvement in working atmosphere was reported by 24; reduction of paid absence by 25; reduction of overtime worked by 1; increased productivity by individuals adjusting hours worked to their own best work rhythm by 17; improved recruitment success by 19; and reduced personnel turnover by 6. Extract from *'Management Today'*.

a) Summarise in not more than 100 words how the flexible working-hours system works.

b) What advantages does the system have
   (i) for employers,
   (ii) for employees?

c) What disadvantages can you foresee?

7. The managers of your company are considering which methods to use for transferring goods. One possibility is using containers. Make a summary in approximately 100 words of the *advantages* of containerisation. Only use the material from the passage below.

One of the chief worries facing any manufacturer is that of ensuring swift, cheap and safe transport for his goods. Consider the problems facing a British factory exporting machinery to Malaysia. The goods must first be taken from the factory, by road, to a railway depot. The railway carries the goods to the docks, where they are stored in a transit shed. Then they are loaded onto a ship. When the ship reaches Malaysia the goods are unloaded. Then they are carried by rail and, later, perhaps by road or even river.

Every one of these steps entails delay, handling expenses, paperwork, and the danger of damage to the goods or pilferage. But consider how a container overcomes these problems. The manufacturer packs his cargo into a tough standard container which fits neatly on to a special crane lifts the container off the trailer and directly on to a flat railway wagon within a minute. The freight train, consisting of perhaps a hundred such wagons, speeds to the docks. Within a couple of hours a massive crane has swiftly lifted each container off its wagon and on to a specially built container ship waiting in an adjacent dock. And so on, whenever the mode of transport changes from road to rail, sea, river or air. The saving in labour is tremendous, and the speed is amazing. Within a single day a container ship can arrive fully laden at a port, unload, reload and leave on her next voyage. Within an hour or two a container train or 'freightliner' can unload and reload.

Containerised cargo is very secure against breakage and theft. The old danger of cargo breaking loose during a storm no longer applies when the ships' holds are completely filled with a neat stack of containers like so many bricks. And the containers need not be sent back to the factory, they can be re-used for different cargo just as a taxi carries passengers from place to place. Imagine a taxi which could use road, rail or sea as it wished, and you have a rough approximation of transmodality, which is the concept of using all methods of transport for a single vehicle. Containers can, in fact, be looked upon as vehicles.

There are some drawbacks to containerisation, of course. Ports need to be equipped with very elaborate and expensive handling equipment, and a container ship cannot use ordinary ports. A small consignment of goods may not be enough to warrant a container.

But the advantages are tremendous for most kinds of freight. The high speed means that the exporter's goods arrive quickly, so that he receives payment sooner, and even the insurance charges are much lower.

8. You work at Phillips and Jones plc as assistant to Mr G Anderson, the Chief Office Administrator, among whose responsibilities is ensuring that adequate administration services are provided for the 150 staff, including mail, typing services, filing and photocopying. Yesterday Mr Anderson had this to say to you:

"Something will obviously have to be done about the photocopier in the print room – it's broken down again. That's five times in the last fortnight! Staff are always ready to complain when this happens but I'm convinced the breakdowns are caused by people not using it properly. I knew we would have this problem when it was agreed to allow staff free access to the wretched machine – people putting the paper in wrongly or being very clumsy using the controls. They don't seem to realise an expensive machine needs careful handling. Apart from this, they don't know how to get the best result out of the machine – not printing on both sides of the paper or reducing A4 sheets on to one. And it's alarming to see how many copies have been thrown away in the waste bin! I've discussed the matter with senior staff and they agree that something has to be done - the present problems will take the whole of tomorrow to sort out and this situation is affecting the general efficiency of the company. It's very inconvenient and frustrating for those who do use the machine properly. I want to send something out to each member of staff today, explaining the situation and get some feedback from them – how often they use it, how many copies they make in an average week, whether they would like some basic training, etc – in fact, any information that may help us to sort the matter out. They may, in fact, want all copying done by a trained operator who can be in absolute control of the machine. If I can have their replies by 15 July, I'll be able to work something out to put to the next senior staff meeting."

Prepare a suitable communication (using about 200 words) for Mr Anderson.

9. You Company has decided to employ three car park attendants, one to work nights and the other two to work alternate shifts from 0730 hours until 1530 hours and 1500 hours to 2230 hours with a one hour break for meals. The night shift will operate from 2200 hours until 0800 hours so that there

will always be somebody on duty in the car park. (The attendants will operate from a kiosk. There will be a barrier at the entrance which can be permanently closed when required) . The applicants should be between 45 and 55 years of age, in good health and capable of working on their own initiative. Anyone with police or armed forces experience would be given priority and enhanced payment is available for either overtime work or duty after 1800 hours. Applications should be made in the applicant's own handwriting to Mr W Collinge. Any holiday arrangements already made will be honoured and wages are by negotiation. These posts will be superannuated and all new employees will be eligible for membership of the company's health and welfare scheme. Holiday entitlement for these posts is three working weeks.

Prepare an advertisement for insertion in the local paper. Select information which you consider relevant from that provided. Credit will be given for good balance and selection of the most important information.

10. Your organisation is about to expand its business with the likelihood of taking on 80 more part-time and full time staff. Prepare a press-release, approximately 200 words in length which is interesting enough to be published in the local press, but whose main motive is to promote your organisation. You may invent any necessary details.

3 Written communication

OBJECTIVES

When you have worked through this chapter, you will be able to:

- — outline the nature and purpose of the memo
- — explain the three possible purposes of a letter
- — state the nature and danger of a personalised circular letter (mail shot)
- — comment on the structure, style and layout of a business letter
- — distinguish between blocked, fully blocked, and semi blocked letter layouts
- — list the main sections of a report
- — state some points to think of when you design a form
- — list the main advantages of word processing over typing.

INTRODUCTION

In business, the first impact one person makes on others is often through words on paper – in the form of a letter, report, memo, or advertisement. This means that in many instances the first – and perhaps the only – opportunity one has to influence others is by one's skill at putting one's thoughts on paper. The most common forms of written communication that one is likely to come across in business are the letter and the office memo. In the day-to-day running of an office it is often essential to inform staff promptly of important facts or instructions. Often a telephone message saves time but the sender cannot be sure that the message will be retained accurately. A written memorandum, in this case, is the most suitable form of communication. However, as this is an open form of correspondence, no confidential information should be included; see Figure 3.1.

Since letters are the most common form of written communication, we shall concentrate at this stage on letter-writing. The same principles, however, apply to all forms of written communication. These principles are concerned with: purpose, content, structure, style and layout (see Figure 3.2).

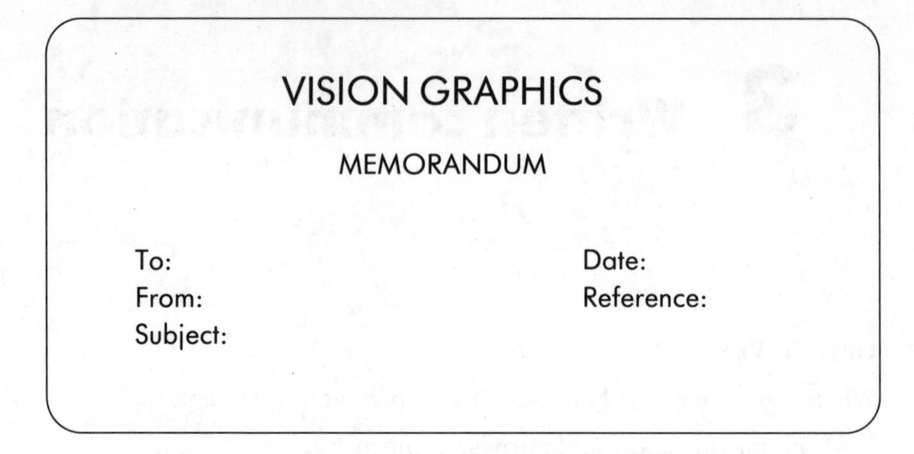

VISION GRAPHICS

MEMORANDUM

To: Date:
From: Reference:
Subject:

Figure 3.1 Sample memorandum

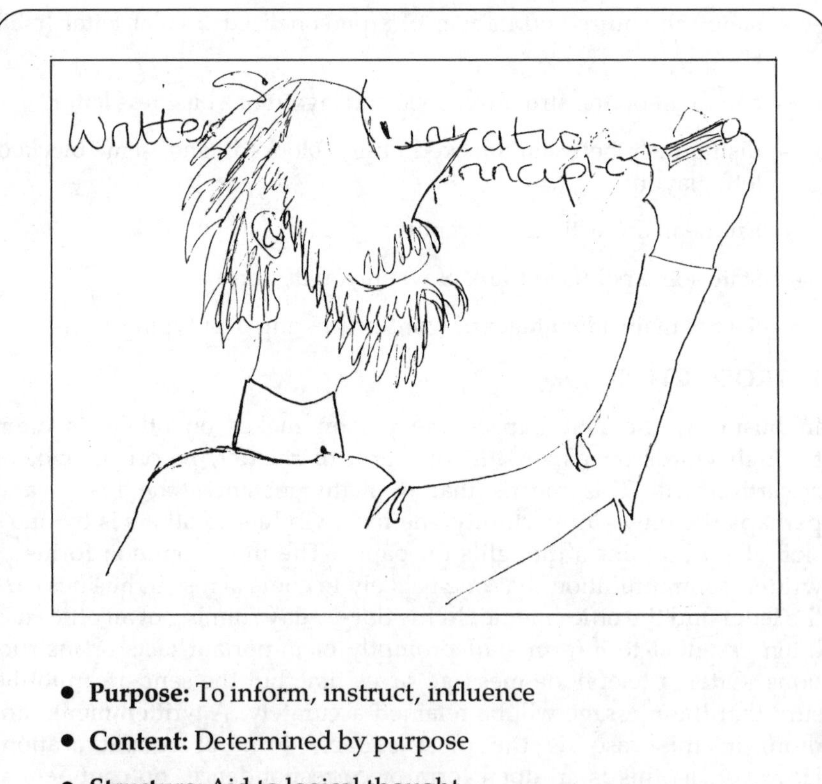

- **Purpose:** To inform, instruct, influence
- **Content:** Determined by purpose
- **Structure:** Aid to logical thought
- **Style/Vocabulary:** Suited to reader
- **Layout/Appearance:** Crisp and clean, reflecting structure

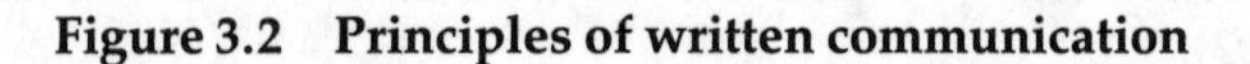

Figure 3.2 Principles of written communication

3.1 PURPOSE

Communications generally, and letters in particular, may have three purposes, either separately or in combination: to inform; to instruct; to influence.

To inform

A letter simply giving information will usually be in response to a request for such, or may be a confirmation or information already provided in another way. Whether the information being given is new to the recipient or is confirmation of information already given, it is in the interests of both sender and receiver that as few words as possible are used (without at the same time giving offence or alarm). Traditional business jargon such as 'your valued communication of 6th ult' or 'may we respectfully draw your attention to' do no more than give the impression that the sender is old fashioned – and old; see Figure 3.3.

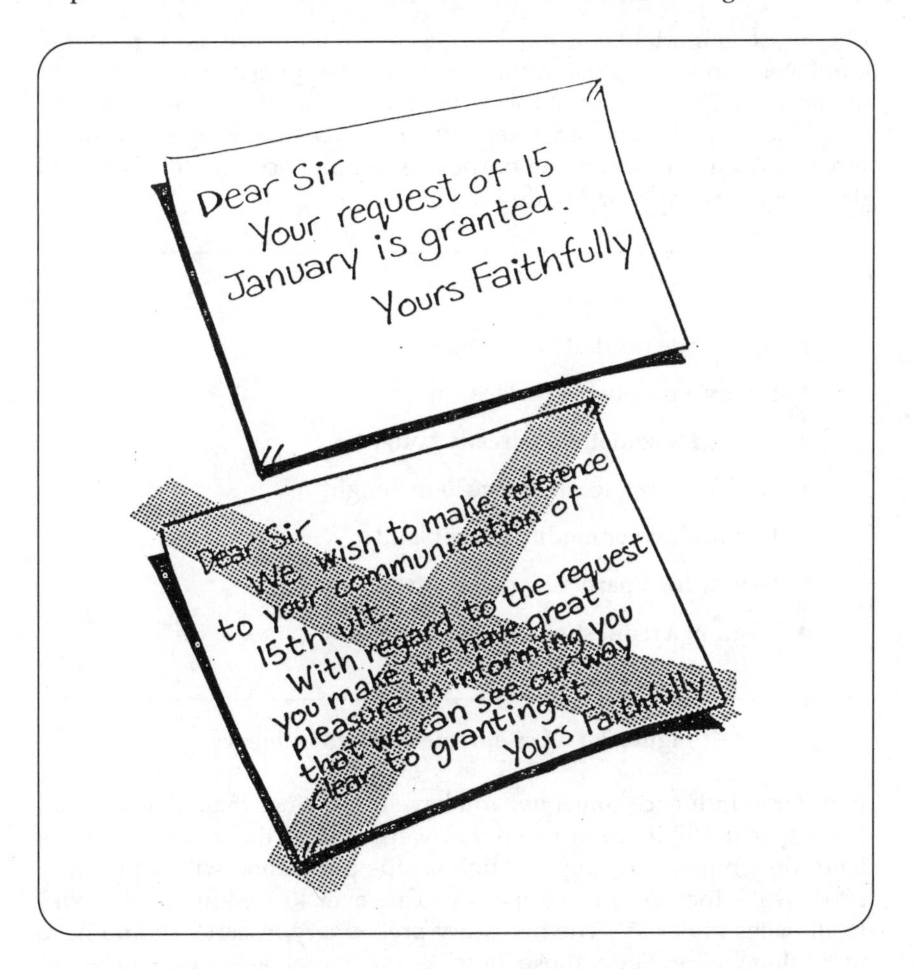

Figure 3.3 Brevity in business communications

Of course not all letters can be as short as these examples. Some matters require delicate handling: a complaint, for instance, about an item of merchandise, or the behaviour of a member of one's family. Even then, there is not excuse for filling a piece of business stationery with meaningless words; this is liable to make the recipient even more cross than before.

To instruct

A letter can do many things: give delivery instructions for goods, call someone up into the army, and so on. The only important things here are clarity and precision. The main content is usually standard, often pre-printed. We are not especially concerned here with this kind of communication.

To influence

The most important person *you* need to influence is a potential employer, and we shall return later to the question of letters of application. The purpose of this kind of letter would be to influence the recipient to grant you an interview. Can you think of some other examples of letters where the purpose is to influence people? – you will find further examples in Figure 3.4.

- To provide needed information
- To buy a product or service
- To pay for something already bought
- To refund/replace defective item bought
- To withdraw or modify a complaint
- To vote for a particular candidate
- To grant a request/permission/interview

Figure 3.4 Letters intending to influence

In order to influence someone, you have to convince them that you had them specifically in mind when you were writing the letter. So a sales letter distributed generally throughout the population will not be very effective if it includes the words: 'if you are over 40', or 'this offer applies to all males under 55'. The necessary preliminary research should have been done to exclude those outside the target age-group or other category from the circulation list. Otherwise the mail-shot will be unnecessarily expensive and will annoy some recipients who might be potential customers for another product or service from the firm.

Many organisations use their computers to produce letters which appear to be personally addressed, often, for instance, scattering the recipient's name at various points in the letter or accompanying literature. This probably influences some recipients positively – just so long as the letter does not begin, 'Dear Mr Smith, if you are over 40...'.

Look at the examples given in Figure 3.5. If you are trying to influence someone, whether to use your product, or to withdraw a complaint they have made, which would be the best way of beginning your first sentence? Can you suggest other better ways? Different people need different treatment of course, but if you do not know your recipient, express your meaning completely and clearly, while paying them the compliment of assuming that they are intelligent and well-informed, without making unwarranted assumptions about their level of knowledge.

- 'you are probably not aware that...'
- 'it can hardly have escaped your notice that...'
- 'as you may well be already aware...'
- 'it must be obvious even to you...'
- 'you are possibly not aware that...'

Figure 3.5 A tactful approach?

3.2 CONTENT

The content depends, of course, on the subject-matter, but it also depends on the level of knowledge and level of need on the part of the recipient(s). As an example, in business it is the normal practice to let colleagues know about correspondence relating to matters or people that concern them. Suppose you are writing to a client on a technical matter, and you have an administrative colleague who you think needs to be informed. The technical letter, while appropriate to the client, may be virtually meaningless to the non-technical colleague. However, rather than sending a separate memo to the colleague, a few words, perhaps hand-written, on a copy of the letter, may be sufficient to convey the level of information needed by the colleague. The MD of the client company, who might also need to be informed, could be sent a copy of the technical letter, attached to another letter explaining why you think he needs to be aware of the contents and drawing his attention to particular aspects.

3.3 STRUCTURE

Any communication should have a beginning, a middle and an end. In the case of a letter, the beginning, in English, is always 'Dear (Sir, Madam, Mr, Mrs, etc)' and the end is usually 'Yours (faithfully, sincerely, etc)'. If you address the correspondent by name, the end choice is usually 'sincerely'; if as 'Sir' or 'Madam', then use 'faithfully'.

The first paragraph should state the reason for the letter. If the letter is intended to influence the recipient, then the opening had better be brief, and of interest (not to you, to the recipient!). The middle should add to the information given in the opening and answer any questions raised there. The ending should state clearly what action you hope or expect the recipient to take as a result of your letter. Examine the sample layout of a business letter shown in Figure 3.6.

1. Company logo
2. Company name
3. Company address
4. Company telephone no
5. References – company and/or recipients
6. Date
7. Addressee
8. Recipient's address
9. Salutation
10. Re:...Subject heading
11. Body of letter ____________________
12. Complimentary close
13. Signature
14. Writer's name printed for clarity
15. Designations/department
16. enc
17. cc
18. Address of registered office, registration details.

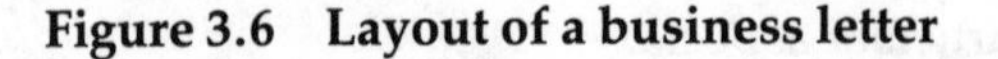

Figure 3.6 Layout of a business letter

Style

Style is something best learned by reading. General rules are: prefer short, concrete, active words to long, abstract, passive ones. Prefer short sentences to long ones. Begin a new line of thought with a new paragraph. Above all, match vocabulary as closely as you can to what you know of the recipient's level of knowledge and education. Examine the sample letter shown in Figure 3.7.

HONEYCRISPS COMPANY LIMITED

Our ref: STJ/FJS
10 August 1992

Shawfield
Birmingham
B21 2KJ

Telephone: 021 473 2121

Mrs S. Fletcher
5 Hillmeadows
Tenderham
Shrewsbury
SR3 6JT

Dear Madam

We were sorry to learn from your letter of 9 June 1992 that you had found a small piece of metal in your packet of Honeycrisps.

We must apologise for this occurrence. It seems that a piece of machinery became loose and small filings from it entered the packing machine. This was discovered almost immediately; however, it seems that some boxes of Honeycrisps were not checked for such foreign bodies. We are grateful that you took the trouble to contact us about this matter.

We enclose with this letter two boxes of Honeycrisps which we hope will compensate you for your distress and inconvenience.

Yours faithfully
HONEYCRISPS CO LTD

S. T. Jones

S. T. JONES
Consumer Relations Officer

encs

Figure 3.7 Sample business letter

Layout

A business letter is normally sent on a printed letterhead. The layout of the printed headings may slightly affect the layout of the letter; most firms also have a 'house-style', with rules on indentation of paragraphs (see Figure 3.8) and position of date, address and complimentary close. Even if you are hand-writing on plain paper, however, decide at the outset what layout you are using and do not change half-way through.

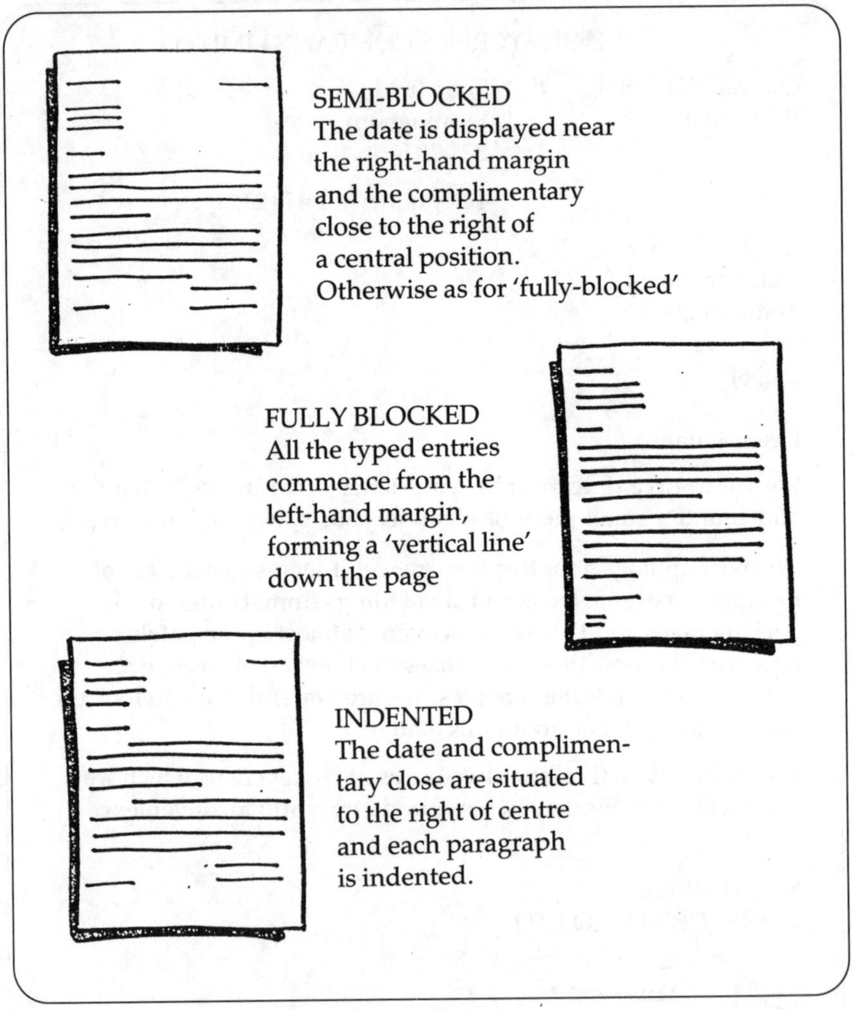

SEMI-BLOCKED
The date is displayed near the right-hand margin and the complimentary close to the right of a central position. Otherwise as for 'fully-blocked'

FULLY BLOCKED
All the typed entries commence from the left-hand margin, forming a 'vertical line' down the page

INDENTED
The date and complimentary close are situated to the right of centre and each paragraph is indented.

Figure 3.8 Letter styles

3.4 DRAFTING A LETTER

To begin with, make notes of what you want to say, or prepare the letter itself in rough form. If you are writing on plain paper, then, unless you have a very good eye, use lined paper underneath as a guide. If you make a mistake, do not immediately start again, because you may make some more later. When you are sure about what you want to say and sure that you have found the right way of saying it, then make a final fair copy. Do not forget the date – people often do. If someone sends you an undated letter, however, do not reply 'With reference to your undated letter'; 'to your recent letter' is kinder.

As a final word on drafting a letter, remember that you may have your letter typed for you. In this case you should either dictate them (often on a dictaphone) or write them out for a typist to copy. If you dictate you must put yourself in the typist's place (ie relying mainly on spoken information), and state exactly where punctuation, paragraphs, etc, should go. If you hand-write your draft, it should be neat and easily read.

3.5 REPORTS

You may from time to time be required to write a report. There are a variety of types of reports, often dependent upon the situation they are required for:

— Routine reports may be asked for on a regular basis, eg your progress report in school or college;

— Occasional reports are often written when something unusual happens, eg an accident;

— Commissioned reports are prepared with a specific purpose in mind. They may be required to investigate a problem that has arisen. They are commonly found in market research projects, eg on types of products or political parties.

Format

There are various possible formats, chosen according to the type of report which may run from a single sheet of paper to hundreds of pages.

— Extended formal reports are used for important issues, often government sponsored;

— Short formal reports are often used as a way to communicate information between middle and senior management;

— Short informal reports are a useful way of conveying more minor information at lower levels within organisations. They do not require the same rigorous attention to style of layout as the more formal report.

How to write a short formal report

Probably the most useful layout to adopt is the short formal report. If the need arises for a more informal style, the formal layout can easily be modified to accommodate this.

First collect the necessary facts and take time to consider their implications, then draw your conclusions.

Sample layout

1 Subject heading ....

2 Report's recipient .... Date.............

3 Report's author..

4 Objectives:	— what the report is about; — who commissioned it; — brief outline.
5 Research methods:	how, where and when you gathered your information, eg interviews, surveys. References to any publications cited.
6 Findings:	state the facts in logical order. Divide the material into numbered sections and sub-sections if necessary.
7 Conclusions:	state the conclusions that you have come to having looked at all the facts. You may also state your own opinion and preferences in this section.
8 Recommendations:	if you feel specific action needs to be taken, you should suggest it at this point.

Style

The style of a report should be factual and objective. As it is never possible to be wholly objective, you should always be aware that some words are more emotive than others and these should be avoided. It is only in the conclusion that you should allow any personal preference to become obvious. In order to promote objectivity in your report you should use the third person throughout, ie 'It becomes evident that...'.

NOW TRY THIS . . .

ASSIGNMENT

In a group choose a topic to investigate and write a report on it.

3.6 FORMS AND THEIR FUNCTION

An important aspect of written communication which needs to be considered is the use of forms. Forms are used extensively in the business world and are also encountered by individuals at nearly every juncture. They are used to record important events such as births, deaths and marriages, they must be completed in order to enrol for a course of study, apply for membership of a club, apply for a job, a driving licence, insurance, to open a bank account or to join a library – the list is endless. The use of forms seems to become more widespread every year. Many people spend much of their working lives completing (or helping others to complete) various types of forms.

Forms can be as simple or as complicated as those shown in Figures 3.9 and 3.10. These are examples of standardised documents which pose questions to elicit specific information. They are efficient in use provided their purpose has been clearly defined and provided they have been well-designed. Clear and precise instructions on its mode of completion should be an integral part of the design of every form. The primary function of a form is to efficiently gather information which, if desired, can be easily collated and analysed. A great deal of thought should go into the design and layout of a form as its effective use within a company can save time and money. The overuse of forms, however, can generate a great deal of unnecessary paperwork which can lead to duplication of effort and consequently to inefficiency. Before considering the introduction of a new form the question should be asked – is it really necessary?

MESSAGE FORM

Time of call .... Date......................................

Name and caller ....

Name and address of firm

....

....

....

Tel. no .... Ext. no ....

Receiver of call ....

MESSAGE:

Taken by ....

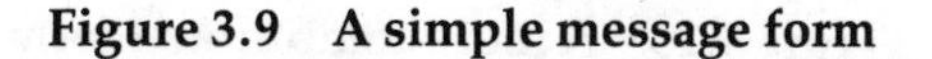

Figure 3.9 A simple message form

Free prescriptions

Form B – P11

Claim on this form if you have a low income

About yourself

Surname (Mr/Mrs/Miss/Ms)	Date of birth	19
First name(s)		
Address		
	Postcode	
Are you in full-time education?	Yes ☐	No ☐
If you are expecting a baby, give the date it's due to be born	Date due	

Who else lives with you?

Give the names of the people in your household, their dates of birth, and say what relationship they are to you, for example, partner parent, son, etc. Include commercial boarders.

Name	Date of birth	Relationship (state if boarder)

- If you or anybody in the list above is registered blind write their names here
- Does anybody in the list above pay you any rent? Write their names here
- Write the names of any children who are still at school full-time
- Does anybody in the list above get Supplementary Benefit? Write their names here

Your housing costs

Put a tick in the box that applies.

If you are a householder
- Do you own your own home? YES ☐ NO ☐
- If you have a mortage, how much do you pay each month? £
- If you pay rent, how much do you pay each week? £ (*Take off any rebate/allowance/housing benefit*)
- Does the rent include heating? YES ☐ NO ☐
- How much of the rent is for heating? £
- Does the rent include lighting? YES ☐ NO ☐
- How much of the rent is for lighting? £

- How much do you pay each year for rates? (*Take off any rebate/housing benefit*) £
- How much do you pay each year for water rates including environment and sewerage charges (if paid separately)? £
- How much do you pay each year for ground rent/feu duty? £

If you live in someone else's home
- What is your relationship to the householder? (*if none, write NONE*)
- If you live there as a boarder, how much rent do you pay each week? £
- Which meals are provided for you? Breakfast ☐ Midday ☐ Evening ☐

Figure 3.10 A more complicated form

Free prescriptions

Form B – P11

Please answer each question and write NONE where the amount is none

Money coming in

Write down the amount of take-home pay coming in each week for
- yourself £
- your partner £

If you get Statutory Sick Pay or Statutory Maternity Pay, write down the amounts here for
- yourself £
- your partner £

Write down the total value of any property (*don't include the home you live in or personal possessions*), savings, and surrender values of life insurance policies owned by
- yourself £
- your partner £
- any dependants £

Do you or your partner get any money from benefits, pensions, or allowances? NO ☐ YES ☐
Write down which they are and say how much you get for each.
- £
- £
- £
- £

Write down how much comes in each week from sub tenants £

Write down any other income £

Money going out

Write down how much goes out each week (*not if already deducted from your pay*)
- fares to work and back £
- child care costs while you are at work £
- superannuation £
- trade union subscriptions £

Write down what items you have on HP and how much your HP payments cost each week (*only include essential household items*)
- £
- £
- £

Write down the cost each week of any life insurance premiums
- self £
- partner/other £

Write down the name of anyone in your family who needs a special diet for health reasons and the nature of the illness
- name
- illness

If your heating bills are high because you or anyone in your family are ill and need extra heating or because your house is difficult to heat, write the reasons below.

Students, if you are in full-time further education, please attach details of your grant and of your term and vacation dates. Also show whether you are making your claim from your term-time or your vacation address.

Declaration

I declare that to the best of my knowledge and belief the information given on this form is true and complete.

Signed Date 19

Warning: to give false information may result in prosecution.

Cut this form from the leaflet and post it to your Social Security office. You can get a pre-paid envelope from the post office.

Designing the form

Having taken the decision to produce a form there are several aspects which must be considered. Because of the great number and variety of forms in use, it is important that they are easily distinguishable from one another and this aspect should be taken into account when deciding on the layout. The following features might be considered:

— colour of paper;

— distinctive border;

— use of logo;

— different typefaces and type styles (eg italic, bold, etc);

— use of space (ie to produce an uncluttered layout and a variety of section sizes to take into account variation in answers).

Instructions on completing the form

Concise, clear instructions should indicate how the form is to be completed and what is to be done with it on completion, eg who should receive it; by what date, etc. It is usually helpful to state whether all sections should be completed, indicating the use of the words 'not applicable' where necessary.

The framing of questions

Once again clarity is all-important. Questions should be phrased in language that will be easily understood by the target group. The form will not fulfil its function if the respondent has to strive to understand the meaning of a question. All 'specialist' language should be accompanied by an explanatory note. Use can be made of direct or indirect questions, eg 'How many children do you have?', 'What are your domestic responsibilities?' Questions should be presented in a logical sequence. A college enrolment form, for example, might present the prospective student with a request to supply the following information: surname; forenames; address; date of birth; previous school; examination results; course required.

NOW TRY THESE...

1. Study a driving licence application form.

Divide into groups. Produce a list of what you think are the most important questions the people who design a driving licence application form need to ask. Put these questions in order of priority.

Now look at an actual application form. Do the questions and their order conform to your list? If not, make a list of those questions you did not include. Do any of these surprise you?

Is the form easy to understand? If not, why not?

2. Now design your own form.

Divide into groups again. Each group should represent the nucleus of a small club. This may be a leisure/sports club, eg badminton, or a hobby club, eg fantasy games. The club wishes to publicise itself in order to attract new members so it decides to distribute information leaflets about its activities with an application form for membership on the back. It is each group's task to design this form.

3. Examine the letter shown in Figure 3.11.

a) On the surface, this letter appears polite. Which words and phrases give this impression?

b) In fact, it is a rude letter which aims at putting Susan in the wrong. Find examples of this.

c) List all the examples of old-fashioned business jargon you can find. Do they always mean what they say?

d) Re-write the letter in such a way that the firm will not reisk losing Susan's custom.

4. Write a letter to the Personnel Manager of 'Associated Cybernetic Systems Limited' applying for the post of trainee programmer. It is an IBM installation and the required programming languages are PL1 and RPG2.

The applications are a mix of scientific, for client companies, and administrative, particularly accounting, for ACSL itself. The job advertisement states that a graduate is preferred. There is a possibility of transfer into systems analysis after 2–3 years satisfactory programming, or, for an expectional candidate, attachment to the consultancy, which operates for clients mainly in the Middle and Far East.

3.7 WORD PROCESSING

The introduction of the word processor to the office environment has not only eased the burden of the hard-pressed secretary, it has changed the environment itself. The necessity to store large quantities of paper documents in cumbersome and space-consuming filing cabinets has been very much reduced. It is now possible to retain vast quantities of information on a hard disk (incorporated into the computer or network), or on a number of floppy disks.

The process of information exchange via a word processor is relatively simple. Each new floppy disk needs to be formatted (a simple procedure), and then data such as letter, reports, circulars, memoranda, etc, can be copied onto the disk and as many hard copies (printouts) as required obtained. Text can be altered with ease – the order of paragraphs, for instance, can be changed if necessary – and different print emphasis, such as the use of bold print, is readily available. It is

2 Low Street
Hoxley HL19 4QZ
Tel. No. Hoxley 5632

Your ref:
Our ref: JPL/MG
6th March 1992

Miss Susan Grant,
3 Mary Hill Road,
Hoxley,
Somerset.
BAS 6LH

Dear Madam,

We are in receipt of your letter of the 28th ult, and the parcel containing the film which you returned.

We deeply regret that you failed to achieve the desired results, but would draw your attention to what we feel sure are instrumental factors in the results you describe.

1. Specific instructions are given which must be followed exactly.

2. Cameras which have not been serviced regularly will not give satisfactory results.

3. Inexperience in video filming techniques may give rise to a poor quality film, in which case, satisfactory results can hardly be expected from our film.

We must emphasise that our products are all thoroughly tested and recommended. Furthermore, we receive thousands of letters from delighted customers in praise of our goods. It is our sincere hope, therefore, that this letter has renewed your confidence in us and that you will continue to use our products in the future.

Assuring you of our best service at all times,

We remain,

Your obedient servant,
VISION GRAPHICS

J. P. Little

JOANNE P. LITTLE

Figure 3.11 Response to complaint

possible, by using a process called 'mail-merge' to produce a personalised letter for circulation to the desired number of clients, however large. Filing is simplified as all information is stored on disk and, provided a security copy of each disk in use is kept, few problems should arise. The word processor facilitates both the distribution and exchange of information and has had a dramatic impact on the business world. Its full potential has yet to be realised.

Read through this case study and think about it. In what ways does it show word processing to be a better form of communication than typing or writing?

Esther Boswell processes words

Esther Boswell owns a small computer consultancy company; both she and her colleague Keith Starsky use word processor systems for the preparation of correspondence, guide booklets and reports. A typical simple session runs like this.

After checking the computer system is properly connected and switched on, Esther inserts her working disk into the drive and "boots" it to start things moving. Booting involves getting the system automatically to set up the word processor function and to carry out two or three introductory tasks. On screen appears the word processor's main menu followed by a list of all the text documents stored on the disk.

Some of these "texts" are standard layouts that Esther uses to give a uniform look to her various kinds of work. Pressing a couple of keys causes the system to transfer a copy of the one she needs for writing reports into the computer's memory. All this takes just a few seconds.

The next stage involves typing in the actual text of the report; Esther has prepared this mentally and has rough notes on paper, so she knows pretty well what she wants to say. So she types with fair confidence, despite using only two or three fingers.

Editing is a fairly straight forward task too. A quick key-press lets Esther jump back to the start of the document; she works through it on the screen, inserting extra material, deleting stray characters as required, and laying it out better. Sometimes she moves a whole paragraph from one part of the text to another. Sometimes she uses special keys to call up task oriented screen menus to help her choose the effects she wants. Sometimes she even transfers in to her new document material from others they have written in the past. She can also call on a spelling checker program to tell her about words that could be wrongly spelt.

The word processor is a WYSIWYG one – "what you see is what you get". This means that at all times the text appears on screen much as it would be printed out on paper. Esther's current document is, however, to be produced in two columns and the WYSIWYG screen doesn't show that. After a while, therefore, Esther turns back to the main menu and asks the system – with another key press – to "preview" the text, to show it on screen properly laid out in double column format. This allows her to take a close look at the overall final appearance of the document. One or two more errors come to light and Esther quickly edits those as before.

The main menu also provides her with the option of pressing a key to tell the system to print a copy of the text in the computer's memory. The printer is a common dot matrix machine tht churns out text in "draft mode" at impressive speed or prints rather more slowly with electric typewriter quality. At this stage, Esther is interested only in seeing a rough draft, so she chooses that option. The text transfers to the printer's own store (buffer), thus freeing the computer for other tasks while the printout is being made.

The author checks the paper draft carefully for final errors and possible opportunities for further polish. After a bit more editing, Esther is satisfied and saves her text as a file on disk for use in the future. This requires a few more simple operations from the word processor's main menu, but takes only seconds. Finally she "locks" the file to make it fairly safe from accidental erasure and instructs the system to print out a high quality copy for their client.

All that work took no more than a couple of hours. During it Esther typed in and carefully edited a seven page document. Since she learned how to use the word processor, she's put all her reports and a number of fairly standard letters onto disk. This is because she realises that she can quickly print any of them out at any time in the future, with or without change. Already she's had some proof of this: they've been able to produce updated copies of some reports at great speed for other clients.

Another major benefit of this aspect of the system is not so obvious. It's that, even after a few more years, Esther could carry the saved masters of all their reports and other such documents around on no more than a handful of floppy disks that cost no more than and take up no more space than a small paperback book. The benefits as regards office organisation will be enormous, they are sure.

The way the office computer system is organised allows other benefits. Both Esther and her colleague Keith use their micro-computers a lot, and not just for word processing. The machines are linked together to form a simple network; each user can easily access the other's files, and they share a hard disc drive as well as having their own floppies to make that straight forward. Because they do not work in the same room, they have a dot matrix printer each; however they plan to buy and share a fast high quality page printer as soon as the prices drop enough.

NOW TRY THESE...

1. You have seen an advertisement for a post of trainee programmer with a firm called Associated Systems Limited. The advertisement merely states that written applications should be made to the Personnel Manager and gives no indication of what form your application should take.

a) State what a suitable application should consist of, AND

b) Write an application on your own behalf using what you consider to be the most effective format or layout.

2. You are asked to make a report to your Department Manager, which may be passed on to higher management if it is suitable, on a piece of computer equipment or a software package with which you have been working.

3. Write a report to your Departmental Manager on a Word Processing package with which you are familiar stating the advantages and disadvantages of replacing the existing typewriter with a Word Processor.

The report should be organised using appropriate headings and sub-headings. You may invent any information or details necessary to enable you to write the report.

4. The Managing Director of your company has been on a tour of the complex and has been annoyed to discover that in the foundry unit he saw workers blatantly ignoring the safety regulations – the non-wearing of safety glasses and protective headgear was the most common.

a) Draft a memo to deal with this problem and state to whom the memo should be distributed.

b) Write a report to the Managing Director recommending measures you would wish to take to improve safety standards in the complex.

5. You have been informed that your Company cannot meet a promised delivery date for a piece of computing equipment to an important customer. There will be a delay of one month. Write a letter of explanation and apology to this customer. You may invent any background information which is necessary for your letter to be realistic.

6. You are the manager of a firm of computing equipment suppliers. Lorries belonging to a firm whose warehouses are adjacent to yours often block your right of way. As manager, write a letter of complaint in a firm but tactful tone, giving a recent instance of obstruction and requesting an end to the inconvenience.

7. You have worked in your organisation for the past five years. Each year you have received a small increment to your salary, but you remain in the same grade. You recently discussed this matter with the Personnel Officer and he asked you to put your request for a salary regrading to him in writing in order that he could take the matter up with the Board. Invent any additional details you think necessary to justify your claim and write a memo to him in which you ask to be placed on a higher grade, thereby gaining an increase in your salary.

8. The firm you work for has a total office staff of twenty. As it is now experiencing some financial difficulties, you have decided to suggest ways in which economies could be affected in the office. Submit your recommendations in the form of a comprehensive memo to the Office Manager, inventing as necessary any details concerning the current organisation and practices of the office.

9. You are a department manager with responsibility for about 200 production-line workers in ten sections, each of which is overseen by a section supervisor. The department closes for the midday meal from 1230 to 1330 but quite large numbers of workers are leaving their machines, improperly, as early as 1215.

The resulting loss of production is becoming serious and your immediate superior has twice expressed his concern at the unauthorised early break. You are aware that the offenders come from several different sections but are unable to be certain that you know exactly which section supervisors are most to blame. Their own production quotas are endangered.

WRITE a MEMO, to be sent to each of your section supervisors, reminding them of the authorised mealtime and asking that the necessary steps to be taken to prevent the loss of production.

10. On September 12 you ordered 12 dozen desk pen sets from the Mitchell Company, to be used as presentation gifts to customers at your company's centenary celebrations on December 20. These units have an excellent quality pen mounted on a white marble base. The cost per unit, including a 3-line message inscribed on the base, was £5.70. All 12 dozen were delivered on December 12, although Mitchell gave you a November 20 delivery date. It was at the time of the late delivery that you noted an error. On every one of the 144 sets the inscription read "Best Wishes from the Sheild Company," instead of "Best Wishes from the Sheald Company".

Because you are 1200 miles from the Mitchell Company, and you wanted these presented on December 20, you rushed them to a local engraver without calling Mitchell. Emory engravers polished the word "Sheild" off and engraved them correctly. This was all done within 24 hours but you had to pay a premium price because of overtime and the difficulty of the polishing job. In any event you have a bill for £216 from Emory Engravers which you feel Mitchell should pay. Write an appropriate letter to the Mitchell Company.

11. The Headteacher of your local High School has written to you to ask if he might bring his Physics Club (48 members) to visit the electronic components department of your company. Unfortunately some of your products are classified as 'secret' by the Department of Defence and tours are not permitted without their official clearance. Write a letter to the Headteacher, regretting that you are unable to comply with this request and explaining why. Perhaps he would like to have his group hear an address by your Research and Development Manager; that can be arranged.

12. Hobson and Brown Limited, who have been good customers of your company Sibor Computing for a number of years, now owe £762. This sum has not been paid within the usual trade terms and a standard reminder has brought no results. Write a tactful letter, including a suitable letter-heading, dealing with the situation.

13. You are the Personal Assistant to the Managing Director of Magnet Limited. There have been complaints from neighbouring firms that Magnet employees have been parking their vehicles, obstructing the entrances and exits to their premises. For some time Magnet have been aware that their own parking area is inadequate and they have obtained adjoining premises with access to a major road which runs behind the industrial estate. It is known that many employees use cars, motor bikes or mopeds and that at least 50 employees use bicycles but exact numbers are not known. Work will start on the new parking area next week and access to the major road will be available in one months time. In the meantime employees are to be asked to park their vehicles carefully until the larger car park is ready. They also need to be told to obtain discs from the Personnel Officer to be placed on their vehicles as they will be asked to display the discs when the new larger area is available. Special stickers will be available for bicycles and when the new area is finished there is to be a specially constructed part for bicycles and light mopeds. Vehicles not displaying authorisation to park will be refused admission or will be immobilised. These appear to be very strict measures but there have been two rather serious accidents at peak times and it takes about 15 minutes to clear the industrial estate at finishing times. Prepare a letter to be sent to all employees giving them the information about parking arrangements. They should also be told that car park attendants are to be employed who will check employees' authority to park vehicles and who will direct vehicles to vacant spaces in the car park. Use any suitable format to ensure good presentation.

14. As Secretary of the professional body to which you belong, write a letter to a well known figure (of your own selection) inviting him or her to address your association at the first of the next season's meetings. In your letter give

some brief introductory details of your association as well as the arrangements for the lecture and for the reception of your speaker, who will be travelling some distance and will have to stay overnight.

15. The large company for which you work, and which manufactures computer equipment, gives substantial sums to charities each year. But it also receives between fifty and seventy letters each month, from schools, churches and so on which are trying to raise money, asking for gifts of equipment which may be sold to swell their funds. Inspite of the merits of the activities of such organisations the company simply cannot meet so many individual requests and must restrict its charitable works to the large annual donations.

PREPARE a GUIDE LETTER on behalf of the company, which might be used in refusing, regretfully, the requests of such individual organisations. Take account of all the circumstances involved.

16. Your firm's social club has a strong membership of older employees but has failed to attract much support from younger members of the firm. As a member of the social club committee write a report for discussion at the next meeting outlining the ways by which you think membership might be increased. Invent as much information as necessary.

17. Your office is burgled, ransacked and vandalised, including serious damage to several items of equipment. Write a report on the incident which will be sent to Head Office. You may invent any necessary details to make the report authentic.

18. The Managing Director of your company has been on a tour of the complex and has been annoyed to discover that in the foundry unit he saw workers blatantly ignoring the safety regulations the non wearing of safety glasses and protective headgear was the most common.

a) Draft a memo to deal with this problem

b) Write a report to the Managing Director recommending measures you would wish to take to improve safety standards in the complex.

You may invent any information or detail necessary to enable you to write the memo and report.

4 Oral communication

OBJECTIVES

When you have worked through this chapter, you will be able to:

- — outline how to prepare a short talk
- — outline how to time your talk
- — explain some ways to make such a talk effective
- — outline the value of visual material
- — list some ways to assess the effectiveness of a talk you attend
- — compare external and internal phone systems and switchboard types
- — outline the use of fax and its problems
- — list the steps in making a phone call
- — design a form for noting phone messages.

INTRODUCTION

Oral communication simply means the use of speech, but in this chapter we are concerned with one-way communication (rather than the normal use of speech, which is in conversation). The use of oral communication of this kind applies to many areas: you may, for instance, be asked to give a talk, you may wish to speak from the floor of a meeting or, slightly less formally, you may have an idea or a point of view which you want to put over to colleagues at work or fellow-members of a social group. In this chapter we also explore using the telephone – talking and making calls. So many people do these badly...

4.1 THE IMPORTANCE OF PREPARATION

However little time you may have for preparation, it is still important to have a plan, otherwise there is a danger that when you stop speaking your listeners will look at each other and say 'What was all that about?' and you will be kicking yourself for having missed out the vital point; having failed to give it proper emphasis; repeating yourself or coming to a stop on a weak point.

You may be able to speak simply using headings that you have first noted down – but check whether these are adequate by first reading your headings into a tape recorder then playing them back. Alternatively, you may feel more comfortable if you first write out in full what you want to say. There is an obvious danger in doing this however: that you will be tempted to keep your eyes directed to your notes rather than to your audience (the easiest way to lose your audience's attention). Even if what you have to say is well-argued and interesting, it may still come across as boring if you do not appear to be interested in your audience. Also, by keeping your eyes on your audience, you are able to sense their mood and so change your style of delivery to match it. To enable you to do this, make sure that key words stand out, by using different lettering, a different colour or underlining. Keep your headings clear of the main text but see that you have enough key words so that even if you lose the thread of what you wanted to say, you can take it up again and still give an effective presentation.

THE PLAN

Introduction

Before giving a talk you will usually have been introduced by the chairman of the meeting, and you can start immediately by saying what you are going to talk about and why (see Figure 4.1). If you have not been introduced, then say who you are and what organisation you represent before moving on to your subject matter. If you are speaking from the floor in a meeting, and if a motion has been proposed, then say whether you are supporting or opposing it. If you yourself are proposing or seconding a motion, then say so.

Main body

Your advance preparation should ensure that you have your points arranged in a logical order, with relevant arguments to support each one.

Conclusion

Summarise the important points you have been aiming to make. If the purpose of speaking is to persuade your audience of something that should be done, then end on a call for action – ask your audience to support or oppose the motion or amendment, contribute to a fund, take part in a campaign and so on. Don't just stop, and don't say something like 'well, my time's up so I shall have to finish'. If time was so restricted then you've wasted what you had by the time you spent on those words. (Similarly, never start by spending time saying you have not been allowed much time and so you will be very brief – it sounds like a way of passing time away and an excuse for not having anything interesting or convincing to say.)

Figure 4.1 A suggested action plan

TIMING

The most important aspect of timing is to make sure you allow yourself enough time for an effective conclusion. You should expect this to take up to a fifth of the total time. Keep a clock in view or put your watch in a place where you can see it (but do not pointedly look at the clock, or at your wrist), and note the time when you will need to begin your summing up.

REVISING

If you have prepared your notes some time before the time at which you are due to speak, it is worth checking them through again after you have been doing something else, to be sure that you have not missed any important points and that the arrangement will allow you to make the presentation interesting. Then, as near as possible to the time at which you will be speaking, read them through again so that the contents will be fresh in your mind.

PREPARING THE SPEECH

To repeat, a talk is only as good as the preparation that goes into it. The more carefully you plan and prepare your speech, the more natural and interesting it will sound. Here are some tips.

Consider your audience

Begin by finding out everything you can about the audience – how big it will be, how sophisticated and knowledgeable, its likes and dislikes. Knowing this, you will be able to talk to the audience on their terms and in the kind of language they prefer.

Collect your material

Collect material for your speech:

— by jotting down all ideas on the subject that come into your mind

— by going to specialists for information

— by selective reading

— by studying any published speeches on the topic.

When you have collected more material than you can use, prune and make a final selection of interesting and relevant points.

Write out the speech in full

Write and rewrite until it comes alive and flows smoothly. Observe the rules of writing for speech which have already been discussed. Give concrete examples of every general point because these add body to the speech. Try to anticipate and answer the audience's unspoken questions. Carefully revise. Add a point here, delete a point there, clarify and polish. Has the speech got a clear structure? This is very important. Without it the audience will have great difficulty in grasping the overall argument. Unlike the reader, the listener can't pause to unravel a point he didn't quite understand. The key to clear structure is logical progression leading to clear conclusions.

Reduce the written-out speech to numbered notes

These will give you the key points one by one, each standing out clearly. After all the preparation, a single word or phrase will be enough to trigger off a whole string of associated ideas.

Finally, rehearse the speech

Don't read from a script or try to memorise your speech because it will sound flat and insincere, and it is the illusion of spontaneity that grips an audience. Use your numbered notes as a guide and find the actual words as you go along. Practise saying the speech in private; listen to yourself on tape to help with pace and diction. If it's not practicable to rehearse aloud, go through the speech quietly building mental sentences from the phrases in your notes.

A large audience has to be passive and it quickly becomes restless unless it is kept entertained. Communication has to be one way – you to them. To compensate for the lack of participation you have to be interesting. A speech doesn't have to be dull if you keep to the following principles:

— Rehearse the speech thoroughly so that a polished performance is assured.

— Spread colour across your subject by using demonstrations and visual aids: the audience's comprehension and interest soar when they see as well as hear the message.

— Show how what you are saying is relevant to or will benefit the listeners: 'If you introduced the following method of cost control you could reduce overheads by as much as 15 per cent.'

— Adjust your speaking speed to suit the audience's reactions. Generally, when speaking to large groups, a disciplined delivery with careful diction and frequent pauses is necessary. Common words, short sentences and several repetitions of the central message all aid communication.

4.2 DELIVERY

If there is a chairman, then face towards him or her as you start. If you are speaking in front of an audience, turn to face them. They should feel that you are looking at each one of them and this will tend to make them feel an interest in you. Stand upright but in a relaxed way, with your weight leaning slightly forward towards the audience; do not lean away from them (Figure 4.2).

- Establish eye contact
- Stand upright, balanced relaxed
- Speak up
- Vary the pace
- Don't fidget
- Don't read
- Allow time for questions

Figure 4.2 Giving a speech

Speak up and don't mumble. It is worth pre-recording yourself and listening for any habitual speech slurring. Don't speak at one pace and on one note, otherwise you will soon have your audience snoring. Try to avoid distracting mannerisms like rattling keys or money or fiddling with spectacles. Keep your hands out of your pockets – concentrate on your subject and your hands will look after themselves. Glance at your notes when you need to: key words and phrases should be sufficiently prominent that you don't have to search for them.

Always look for audience reaction to what you are saying – the occasional *ad lib* to take advantage of these reactions can add greatly to the interest. If a member of the audience wants to ask a question, respond positively. Provided you have properly prepared your material, you should be able to capitalise on questions by giving effective answers – but be careful not to be thrown too far off your timing.

When the speaker is confident or appears to be confident the audience, by reflection, feel a heightened confidence in what he says. And it is remarkably easy to deceive an audience. Even when you are very nervous it is easy to disguise the fact by adopting an erect posture, a steady gaze and a deliberately clear voice. Diffidence and nervousness don't matter provided they are not communicated.

'The jitters' are perfectly normal – even very experienced speakers get them. But after a few minutes on your feet they usually go away and you start to enjoy the experience. Nerves can raise or ruin your performance – it all depends on how well you control them. A good opening tactic is to drain some of the tension out of the atmosphere by cracking a joke or telling an amusing anecdote. Another way of controlling nerves is to take out a handkerchief, fold it carefully, tuck it in your breast pocket – while waiting for the inner turmoil to subside.

Even if your nerves do show and you start to stutter and stumble, don't worry too much. Every person in the audience is used to stuttering and stumbling in ordinary conversation and probably won't even notice your own slips.

Key points

1. When writing the speech use signposting techniques – eg listing at the beginning the main points to be covered. This makes it easier for the audience to follow your argument and breaks the mental journey into short and easy stages.

2. Place strong material – your most important and interesting points – near the beginning of the speech: audiences soon flag and the material they hear while still alert makes the greatest impact.

3. Audiences prefer a two-sided or all round presentation.

4. When writing your speech, collect more material than you need and

prune. Write out the speech in full from this final selection of material, then reduce this draft to numbered notes.

5. With large audiences the communication has to be one way – you to them. Since participation is ruled out they have to be kept entertained, otherwise they quickly become restless. So rehearse the speech carefully to assure a polished performance and use visual aids, demonstrations, etc to add interest.

6. Small audiences enjoy participating through discussion and question and answer. Thus an informal and flexible approach by the speaker is necessary.

7. To control stage fright

- — while waiting for the nerves to subside; try folding a handkerchief;
- — try to drain some of the tension out of the atmosphere with a joke or anecdote;
- — adopt an erect posture, steady gaze and deliberately clear voice: most audiences are fooled by appearances.

4.3 SUBJECT MATTER

If you have a choice of subject matter, then select a topic which interests you and for which you can display enthusiasm (Figure 4.3). If you don't already have the necessary knowledge, then research your subject beforehand. If you are planning to make any assertions, then make sure you have the appropriate evidence to hand, possibly with quotations.

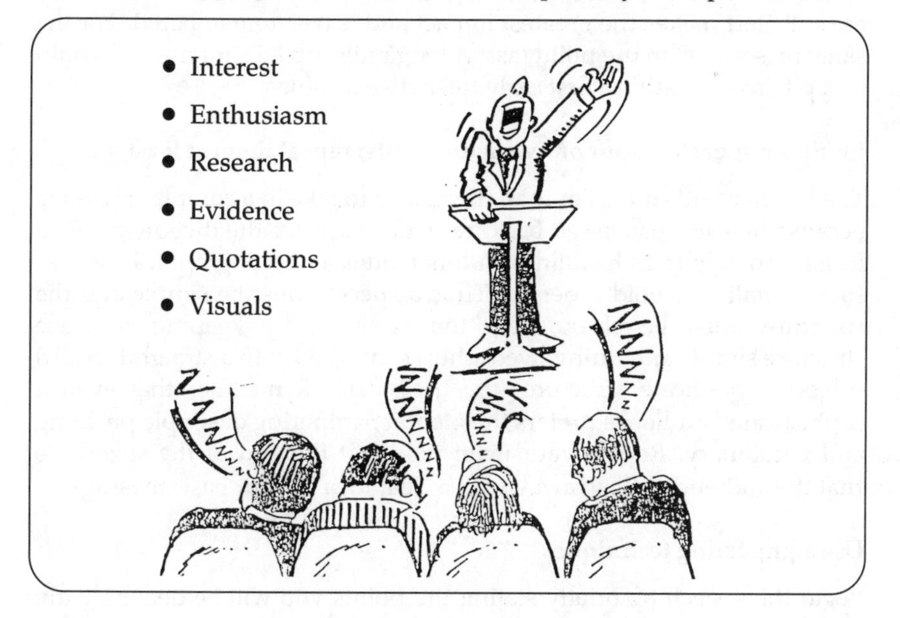

Figure 4.3 Selecting subject matter

Remember that more information tends to be taken in through the eyes than through the ears, so if there is something relevant that you can give the audience to look at – so long as it supports what you are saying and is not distracting – then any time spent in the preparation of visuals will not be wasted. Even something that the audience can't see can arouse interest, as for instance if you hold up a document which illustrates or emphasises your point and say: 'I have in my hand the following...'.

4.4 MORE PRACTICAL ADVICE ON PUBLIC SPEAKING

Keep the speech short

Research indicates that listeners' retention drops severely after fifteen minutes' straight talk and reaches saturation point after thirty minutes. It might be helpful if you wrote in a sentence at the beginning of the speech to the effect that you intend to keep the speech short to allow more time for questions afterwards. In any case, most speakers are more interesting when answering questions than when lecturing.

Because of this factor there will be no room for elaborate introductions or other formalities so keep these elements out of the speech. To save time, make abrupt transitions from one topic to another. The audience won't mind. They are used to abrupt transitions on television news and current affairs programmes.

Place strong material at the beginning of the speech

The most important and interesting points should be made early in the speech because audiences soon flag. The material they hear while they are still alert makes the greatest impact and is best remembered. For the same reason, get to the point fast. A long build-up kills interest. It would be a pity to waste those first early, receptive minutes.

Limit the speech to four or five main points; repeat them at least once

The listener finds it harder than the reader to take in a complex message because he can't pause, go back, re-read, reach for the dictionary. And he gets no help from headlines, sub-headings and typographical devices such as italics or bold typeface. Thus a speech must be simple and the structure must be clear. Help the audience by keeping sentence structure simple and uninvolved, short sentences with a straightforward subject – predicate structures are the safest. Remember that even a sophisticated audience prefers the mental pampering of simple phrasing and vocabulary. Repeat your main points at the end of the speech so that the audience will go away with a clear idea of your basic message.

Use signposting techniques

Begin the speech by briefly stating the points you will be dealing with: 'First I shall examine the Government's policy in this field: then deal with... and finally...' This device will help the audience to follow your argument and to see the structure of your speech. It also motivates them to listen by breaking the mental journey into short and easy stages.

Make the speech looser and gentler-paced than you would if writing for publication

Most good speeches look loose and repetitive when transcribed to paper. Published language is usually tight and compressed and highly organised. When spoken aloud it creates comprehension problems for the listener, who can't ponder and re-read. So make a few points only and take your time in making them.

State the opposing point of view

A heavily biased, one-sided presentation will be well received only if the audience is unsophisticated and unlikely to meet with later counter-arguments. A two-sided or all-round presentation is the best tactic when dealing with a controversial subject. Such an approach is preferred by most audiences since it implies honesty and objectivity.

Begin with opinions with which the audience will agree

This increases the audience's confidence in the speaker so that they listen with more respect to the rest of his speech, including the parts which counter their own opinions.

Make sure the speech will sound right

Practise saying it aloud and listen to the results on tape. Are there too many s's or b's clustered together? Are there any awkward-sounding phrases or word combinations? Do you sound enthusiastic and interesting? Are there too many ums and ers and 'I mean'? If so, you could eliminate most of these by slowing down and speaking more deliberately.

NOW TRY THIS...

Materials needed: cards with names of characters and roles.

Student activity:

- drawing up an agenda;
- taking minutes;
- presenting speech to meeting.

You are presented with a hypothetical situation, eg a proposal to build a motorway in your area. You are each provided with a card and expected to take on the role it describes. You must prepare a three-minute speech from the information given on the card. However, you may bring in any extra points which seem to be relevant. You must then present this speech at a simulated formal meeting. Other students will act as an audience and they must be prepared to ask questions (which you must then answer), and to take part in a discussion. Students should also draw up an agenda and take minutes of this meeting.

If possible, these speeches should be recorded on video and played back so that you can assess your own performance. Other students (or your tutor) can assess each speech on a form similar to the one in Figure 4.4.

Assessment criteria

Speech and discussion – possible score 85%

Mark for: the ability to present a clear and well structured speech; clarity of voice; organisation of content and an understanding of the conventions of a formal meeting.

A *credit grade* should be given to students who show insight into the situation – who attempt to use the vocabulary and attitudes of the role given to them and who bring in sensible background detail. They should also show diplomacy in handling opposition to their viewpoint both in their speech and in the subsequent discussion.

A *fail* should be given to students whose speech is incoherent, who have made no effort to enter realistically into the role and who make no attempt to enter into the discussion.

Agenda and minutes – possible score 15%

Students should show a knowledge of the formal rules and terminology of drawing up agenda and minutes. They should show ability to select main points from the meeting for inclusion in their minutes.

The assessment process

Introduction

- — Did the talk have a title and was it made clear at the outset how much of the subject would be covered?
- — Was the introduction sufficient to enable the listener to follow the theme of the talk?
- — Did the speaker try to create interest in his subject?
- — Was enthusiasm for the subject displayed?

Presentation

- — Was material presented well or badly?
- — Was material arranged in logical sequence or was it disjointed?

Evaluation Table	Un-acceptable	Weak	Acceptable	Good	Very good
1. Preparation: Knowledge of/analysis of problem Knowledge of background Knowledge of audience Arrangement of facilities (ie suitable room, visual aids)					
Comments:					
2. Presentation: Personal – appearance – manner – vocal clarity – vocal modulation					
Comments:					
3. Material – introduction – findings – conclusions – summary of recommendations – detailed recommendations – final conclusion, if any					
Comments:					
4. Overall reaction: Awareness of audience Reaction to feedback Opportunity for questions					
Comments:					
5. Final grading on overall impressions:					

Figure 4.4 Assessment form

— Did the speaker show a knowledge of the subject?
— Did the talk show evidence of research?
— Did the talk have a beginning, a middle and an end?
— Did the speaker show any defects in presentation?
— Was the speaker fluent? (ie were such expressions as '-er', 'you know', etc, avoided?)
— Was the overall pace too fast or too slow?
— Were there variations of speed?
— Was there a variety of intonation and style?
— Were there any distracting mannerisms?
— Did the speaker try to display confidence?
— Did the speaker try to establish eye contact with the audience?
— Did the speaker try to use any visual aids to assist in the presentation?
— Was the speaker capable of competently handling questions from members of the audience?
— What was your overall impression?

4.5 TELEPHONE TECHNIQUE

Answering the telephone is an important duty because when you are working in an office you are representing your firm and the tone of your greeting and the manner in which you handle the calls create a favourable or unfavourable first impression.

Telephone systems

There are three main kinds of telephone system and various interconnecting devices which facilitate the task of oral communication by telephone.

Internal

On internal telephones you are able only to talk to people inside the firm by means of another telephone extension. You cannot make outside (external) telephone calls.

External

On external telephones, you can dial external telephone numbers only.

Both

On some telephone systems you can dial internal extensions as above, but if you have to make an external call you are able to get an outside line. Often this is done by first dialling 9 to connect you to the dialling tone for the outside line.

Switchboards

In a firm which has several extensions a switchboard is necessary to receive and route the incoming calls to the required person or department. There are two main types:

PMBX – an abbreviation for private manual branch exchange – is a system in which the telephonist makes all the connections between the extension users and the incoming and outgoing calls.

PABX – an abbreviation for private automatic branch exchange – is a system whereby the extension users may dial their own calls; the switchboard operator, however, must receive and route incoming calls.

Answering machines

If you wish to provide a 24-hour telephone service you may connect the telephone to an answering machine. This gives a pre-recorded announcement, perhaps asking the caller to leave a message on tape.

Recording machines are common in offices and, indeed, now appear in more and more homes. They are very cheap and many people think them essential. Yet they aren't everywhere – why not?

There is no doubt that many people are frightened to leave a message on an answering machine. Perhaps they are surprised not to be able to speak to a person: often the lack of feedback puts them off. They may leave no message at all, or may become almost incoherent. Sometimes the message that greets callers can confuse them too. On the other hand, that message gives you time to collect your thoughts and decide on what to say. When communicating with an answering machine, be clear, precise and brief. Say who you are, the time of your call, the person to whom you want to speak, your message – and your own phone number.

Many owners of answering machines are just as bad! They prepare poor messages; they don't listen to the tape for a long time; they don't call back. Maybe they are frightened of the technology too? or maybe they do not want to pay for a follow up call. That gives a very bad impression to callers – and may lose you clients.

The most important other system people can link to a phone line is a fax system. This allows you to send a message that would otherwise be on paper (a memo, letter or drawing for instance), cheaply and quickly. Some systems take output straight from a computer; the more common fax machines scan the sheet you feed through and send an electronic

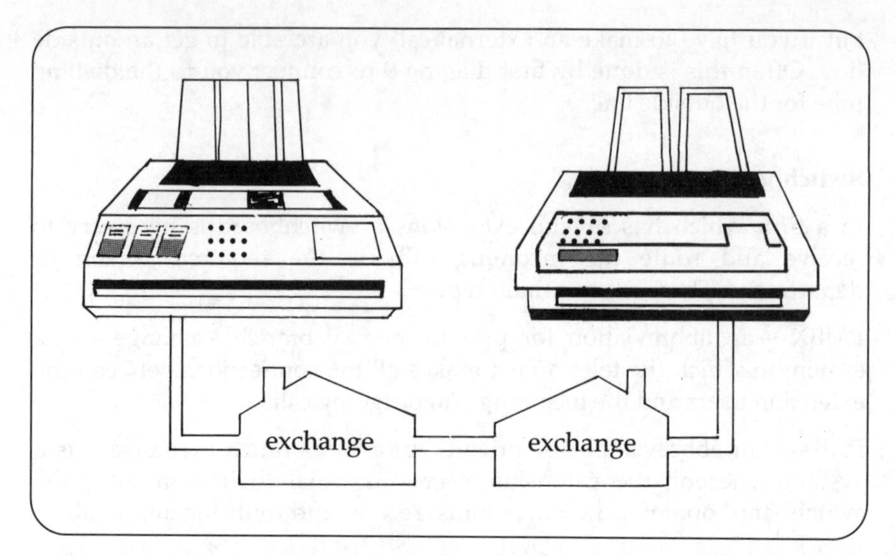

Figure 4.5 For fax you need a channel between the sending and the receiving machines

copy through the phone network. At the other end a similar computer or fax machine decodes the data and produces a copy for the other person to read.

Fax systems are now remarkably cheap for what they can do, and many people use them more than the phone. They are of particular value for sending messages quickly when the other person is not around (maybe the office is across the world and is closed) or is too busy to speak on the phone.

Electronic mail is another modern approach to speedy communication, while some firms still use the very costly telex system.

NOW TRY THESE...

1 Find out what types of telephones your college uses. How do you make an external telephone call from the college? Find out what type of switchboard is used.

2 You are asked to ring a local florist to order flowers for the manager's office. When you telephone, you hear a recorded message which says: 'Bournville Florists. Thank you for your call. The shop is closed for lunch. If you wish to leave a message it will be dealt with this afternoon. Please give your name, address and telephone number and speak slowly and clearly. Begin your message now...' Write down the message you would leave, making your answer clear and concise.

3 Find out how many telephone reference books there are and what their specialities are.

Look in the front pages of your local telephone directory and find the names of the recorded services available to subscribers. Find the telephone number of each recorded service (the centre nearest to you) and work out the cost for a one minute call to each one.

Find the following telephone numbers:

— the local bus station;

— the nearest main line train station;

— the local library;

— the nearest information centre;

— the local police station.

What number should you dial in an emergency? Name the emergency services.

Operating the telephone

Before you begin to dial a number you should make a note of all the information you may need in order to make an efficient telephone call. Be prepared for various turns in the conversation and collect your thoughts and all necessary paperwork beforehand. The telephone call record shown on page 71 gives an example of useful information planning memo that you may want to use. When you are ready, make your telephone call keeping in mind the following points:

— make sure you have the correct number and dial carefully;

— try to make long distance calls during the cheap rate periods if they are not urgent;

— do not agree to hang on if you cannot be put through straight away;

— keep the conversation brief, concise and to the point.

Speak clearly when making or receiving a call. When answering the phone always say 'Good Morning' or 'Good Afternoon' as appropriate and state the name of your company. Never be rude or too familiar with the telephone callers. For example, if the person who your caller wants is out, neither have a long chatty discussion about it nor dismiss their enquiry with a curt 'He/She's out'. The polite response is to ask if you can take a message. For this reason it is always useful to keep a pen and a message pad by the telephone and to observe the following list of appropriate responses:

— answer promptly;

— find out who the caller wants to speak to;

— do not leave the caller waiting without conveying what action you are taking;

— always be polite, sympathetic and remain calm, even if subject to verbal abuse;

— if you cannot connect the caller immediately, offer alternatives such as to phone back later (meanwhile take a note of the caller's telephone number); to be connected to another person likely to be of assistance or to take a message.

NOW TRY THIS...

Arrange with your tutor to make an internal phone call. You wish to telephone Mr Lynch, the environmental health officer, to ask him to come and advise the staff how to deal with a wasp's nest that has been found just outside the main entrance. After you have made this call, record the appropriate details on the 'Telephone Call Record' sheet, given in Figure 4.6.

NOW TRY THESE...

1. Protech Software Limited is launching a new word processing package. As a product manager you are required to give an introductory speech to a conference which is attended by eminent people from industry. Draft a short speech keeping in mind the plus points of the product.

2. a) Select an item of computing equipment or a software package with which you are familiar and draft a short speech to be delivered to a group of potential customers.

   b) What factors would you take into account when giving the speech to ensure that it was effective?

3. A firm is considering computerisation. You have been retained as their consultant to implement the project. Management fully supports this proposal but some of the staff are a little apprehensive. You have been asked to give a speech to all the employees on the benefits of computerisation in order to obtain their full co-operation. Describe how you would go about preparing the speech, what points you would include and what factors you would keep in mind about delivery.

4. Your employer is concerned that not all staff are displaying good techniques when talking to customers on the telephone. He has asked you to:

   a) draft a letter or memo to be sent to all staff, which details examples of good practice which he wishes them to follow;

   b) design a telephone message form, with appropriate headings, to help those taking calls to record all necessary details.

5. a) What information should appear on any record of a telephone message?

Date and time of call	
Name and address of Organisation	
Telephone number	
Extension	
Name of person you want to speak to	
Your name	
Where you are from	
Why you are phoning	
What you want to know	
Information obtained	

Figure 4.6 Telephone call record sheet

b) How should you answer the telephone when:

(i) an external call is transferred to you from the switchboard?

(ii) an external call comes directly through to you?

(iii) a call which your supervisor (who has just left the room) requested comes through from the switchboard?

6. a) Draft a short speech (four to six minutes) which is to be delivered to a group of managers at a company for which you work. The object of the presentation is to attempt to secure their approval for the purchase of a new piece of office equipment. Keep in mind that they are concerned with expenditure and need 'hard' proof to be convinced. You may invent any background information which is necessary for your presentation to be realistic.

b) What factors would you take into account when making the presentation to ensure that it is effective?

7. Your superior has to attend a sales conference at which she is to present a new product to potential buyers. (You may choose, as the produce concerned, any piece of computer equipment or software with which you are familiar or which you think might be developed in the near future.) As pressure of work is very high she has asked you to help by evaluating the product and then drafting TWO documents for her to use: -

a) The sales promotion speech she is to give.

b) A sheet of notes as to what she should do in order to make the presentation as effective as possible.

8. Consider the following notes of a telephone conversation. In it the secretary makes *ten* major errors: identify and briefly define each error.

The scene is the Sales Manager's office. He is out. The telephone rings and his secretary answers it.

Secretary: Hello.
Caller: Can I speak to the Sales Manager, please?
Secretary: No, I'm sorry, he is out.
Caller: Who is that speaking, please?
Secretary: His secretary.
Caller: Oh! Well, I wonder if you can help me.
Secretary: Yes?
Caller: I put in an order for six hundred of your BX45 six weeks ago and I have not yet received them. The order number is 456940 and your invoice number is 005746.

Secretary: Just a second. I'll have to get a pencil and paper.

(She puts the receiver on the desk and fetches a pencil and a piece of scrap paper).

Secretary: Hello, I've got something to write on now. Give me the information again.

Caller: Six hundred BX45 ordered six weeks ago. Order number 456940; your invoice number 005746.

(Secretary writes furiously)

Secretary: Just a moment. What was the order number?

Caller: 456940

Secretary: And the invoice number was 5746?

Caller: No!! 005746

Secretary: O.K. I've got that.

(knock on the door)

Secretary: Come in.
(Jane enters) Hello, Jane!
(To caller) Hang on, please
(To Jane) Shan't be long, but Mr James is out and I've got to deal with his calls.
(To caller) Was there anything else?

Caller: Well, I want to know when I can expect delivery. Can you get Mr James to ring me?

Secretary: All right, but he won't be in till late this afternoon.

Caller: I shall be in until 5.30.

Secretary: I'll ask him to ring, then. Good-bye.

(She notes something on the paper)

(She replaces the receiver, leaves the paper on her boss's desk and goes out of the room with Jane)

The message reads: '6 hundred BX not sent. Their order 456940 Invoice 005746. Please ring today re delivery.'

9. What in your opinion are the main problems which arise when people are not well trained in the use of the telephone and how do you think they could be avoided?

10. There have been many complaints recently, from suppliers, customers and the general public, that telephone communications with your company are poorly dealt with.

a) Why is it important that telephone calls should be dealt with carefully?

b) In what ways can calls be dealt with badly?

c) What special attitudes and skills need to be encouraged and developed in order to communicate well by telephone?

d) What, if anything, can be done about the small minority of employees who, by voice or manner, seem doomed to offend callers.

5 Applying for a job

OBJECTIVES

When you have worked through this chapter, you will be able to:

— explain how an employer with a vacancy deals with applications

— produce a letter of application for a job

— comment on how to approach an application form

— state the nature and purpose of a curriculum vitae and list the main contents.

INTRODUCTION

Getting a good job that you can do well and will enjoy may be the most important thing in your life! The last stage is the interview, which demands many stages of face to face communication. We'll come to interviews in the next chapter. Now we will see how written communication skills are of great importance in getting you to that interview. In particular we look at letters and application forms.

5.1 LETTER OF APPLICATION

One letter, the one that lands you your first job, can totally change your life – so never let an application go until you are satisfied that you cannot improve upon it.

The sifting process

Put yourself in the position of the employer who has just advertised a vacancy; the letters start pouring in. There could be 20 or 200 letters of application for a single job. Out of all these, the employer has to pick just 5 or 10 to ask to an interview. What would *you* do? How would *you* pick out the small handful which 'win' at this stage of the competition, and get invited to an interview? Let us look at ways in which you can try to get your own letter among the winners.

The first throw-out

To begin with the employer does not think about the 'good' letters. His first interest is the *bad ones* – the ones he can throw straight into the bin.

Firstly he will throw out any letters that are dirty and badly written. Remember, he *wants* to find an excuse for throwing all but a handful away, so any excuse will be pounced on and that letter will end up in the rubbish bin (see Figure 5.1).

The second throw-out

An employer will then go through the letters again, throwing out some more, until he has about twice the number that he wants to interview left. At this stage, he will keep only the letters which satisfy the following criteria:

- they are not too long;
- they give relevant information about the applicant;
- they avoid any attempt to show off;
- they are not vague and wordy, or give unnecessary information.

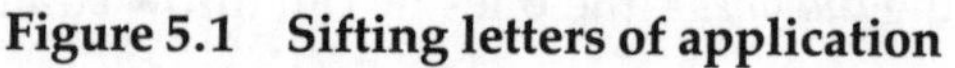
Figure 5.1 Sifting letters of application

Short list

Finally, the employer will go through the pile a third time, and this time he will be looking for something positive, that certain 'something' that says 'This person seems to be good; the kind of person we ought to ask to an interview'.

The essentials

So how do you avoid both the 'throw-out' stages shown above and get through to the short list (Figure 5.2)? Many letters of application miss the most obvious points – even the applicant's address. Make sure you include all the following essentials:

— the address where you can normally be contacted, at the top, with a phone number if possible;

— the date;

— the address of the firm you are writing to;

CONTENT

- Your address, phone number
- Firm's address, name of person
- Post applied for
- Clean opening and closing sentences
- Relevant experience, qualifications
- Own name written clearly
- One side of paper
- Clean and tidy

Figure 5.2 Presentation of application

— if you know the name of the person you are writing to then either address him or her directly or put 'For the attention of Mr/Mrs/Ms ...';

— indicate the post you are applying for;

— give clear opening and closing sentences;

— give details of previous experience and employment – perhaps in the form of a separate curriculum vitae (see below);

— show how you can meet the stated and hidden requirements of the job (but do not apologise for experience or qualifications you *do not* have);

— keep it short. If your application letter is too long employers might not read it at all. Avoid unnecessary details unless they are specifically asked for and include only the things that would interest *you* if you were the employer;

— aim to fill one side of an A4 sheet of paper and no more;

— print your name underneath your signature.

Make sure the whole letter is clean, clear and tidy, without any crossings out or mistakes. When you make your first mistake do not begin the letter again; keep going because you are bound to spot other weaknesses; so let your first attempt be the rough version. Study the checklist shown in Figure 5.3 before trying to compose your letter.

5.2 APPLICATION FORMS

Some employers may require you to fill in an application form like the one shown in Figure 5.4. If an advertisement specifies this, simply write or phone for the application form and fill it in rather than wasting your time composing a letter of application. As an exercise, read the form carefully, then fill it in.

The questions

Some of the questions on a printed application form may seem pointless – your hobbies, for instance, or whether you are married. You must assume that the employer has a purpose in asking them.

Experience and education

Application forms usually allow a certain amount of space for these details. First see what is required, then write it out on scrap paper to make sure you have the information in the correct order and that you will be able to fit it into the space available. Remember the importance of 'first impressions'.

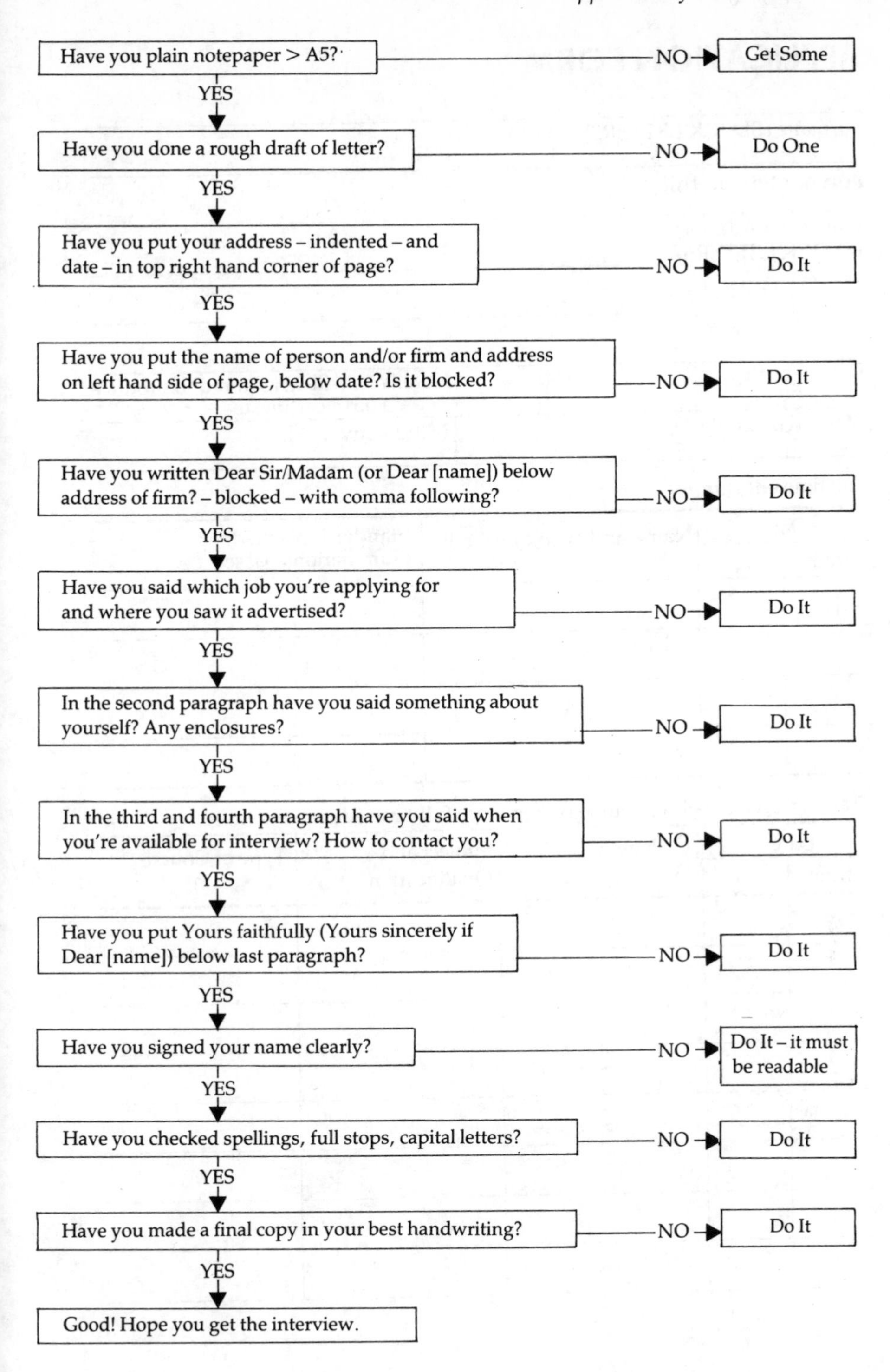

Figure 5.3 Application checklist

APPLICATION FORM

Surname (BLOCK LETTERS)

Forename(s) in full

Full Postal Address
(BLOCK LETTERS)

Date of birth

Note: You will be required to produce a birth certificate

Married or single

Nationality

Full time education

Date		Name and type of school	Standard reached, examinations passed
from	to		

Training Give details of courses taken since full-time education ceased

Date		College	Subject and Qualification	Type of Course
from	to			

Figure 5.4 Application form

Full particulars of your Employment over the last 4 years

Names and addresses of Employers	Dates		Duties	Reason for leaving
	from	to		

Health	Office use only
Have you suffered from –	
fits	
rupture	
any other serious illness	
any accident	
If registered under The Disabled Persons Act 1944 give Reg. No.	

Leisure interests (hobbies, sports, clubs etc.)

The information I have given above is true to the best of my knowledge and belief

Signed________________________ Date________________

For official use	
Suitability (Tick appropriate box.)	highly suitable probably suitable suitable unsuitable
comments covering experience, special qualities etc.	

Appearance

Write neatly using pen, not pencil. Print if your normal writing is uneven or untidy. If the form says 'use capitals', then make sure you do.

Completeness and correct spelling

Ask someone else to check your completed application form before sending it in. It is easy to miss something out without noticing. Employers also place a lot of importance on correct spelling – even judging poor spelling to be an indication of low intelligence – something which is not necessarily the case.

Completion of an application form at the employers' premises

If you know you are going to have to fill in a form when you arrive for interview, prepare a CV (curriculum vitae – see below) beforehand, then have it checked as above. Carefully check your entries on the form against those of the original before handing the form in. Your CV will also serve as a source of information to ensure that you have missed out nothing important.

Why you want the job

Application forms may contain a section asking for further relevant information about yourself and about your reasons for wanting the job. You should think carefully about how your abilities, interests, training and experience match the needs of the job, and why you want the job. Those who make the best of this opportunity are the ones most likely to be invited to an interview.

5.3 CURRICULUM VITAE

In order to keep a letter of application short and readable, it can be a good idea to prepare a separate CV. (The phrase means 'story of your life', but people want to find only certain types of information, as we shall see.) It will also save you a lot of work if you need to apply for several jobs before you get a firm offer. Make sure the CV is clearly laid out and keep its length to two sides of a page at most – one side is preferable (see Figure 5.5).

NOW TRY THIS...

Prepare your own CV using the suggested layout given.

NOW TRY THESE...

1. If possible, work in groups of five or six.
Pretend you are the bosses. You are going to choose a new employee for your firm. Decide what kind of job it is and what the new person will

CURRICULUM VITAE

Name:

Address:

Tel No:

Date of birth:

Age: (in years)

Sex:

Status: Single/Married

Education:

____________	School	Year-Year
____________	College	Year-Year
____________	University	Year-Year

Public examinations:

Level	Subject	Grade	Subject	Grade
		"	"	"
	"	"	"	"
Level	Subject	Grade	Subject	Grade
	"	"	"	"
	"	"	"	"
Level	Subject	Grade	Subject	Grade
	"	"	"	"
	"	"	"	"

Degree(s) and/or other post-school qualifications:

Postgraduate qualifications:

Work Experience:

Full-time work:

1) Position	Firm	Date–Date
2) "		
3) "		

Part-time work:

1) Position	Firm	Date–Date
2) "		

Hobbies and Interests:

Referees:

Academic:	**Character:**
Name	Name
Position	Position
Address	Address
Tel No.	Tel No.

Figure 5.5 Suggested layout of a curriculum vitae

have to do. When you have done this, prepare an advertisement for the rest of the class to respond to.
Here are some words you might need:

applicant	permanent	confidence
qualifications	temporary	proficient
experience	competent	enthusiastic
clerical	assistant	position

When you have finished, one member of your group's 'Board of Directors' should write your advertisement on the board.

2. Everyone in the class should now write letters of application for the jobs advertised by the different groups. If possible write applications for two or three different . Use *false names throughout* so that each application can be judged on its merits. Send your letters.

3. Each 'Board of Directors' not sorts the applications for 'your' advertisement to decide which applicant you want to interview – you should also choose one 'reserve' candidate.

4. Under the heading **'How We Chose Our Candidate'**, answer the following questions:

— What made you choose your 'best' candidate – his or her age; qualifications; handwriting; address; interests; some other factor?

— What made you reject some of the candidates – their handwriting; spelling mistakes; length of letter; an obvious inaccuracy; some other factor?

— Make some suggestions for things an employer would look for when he reads a letter of application, and how he would choose his short list.

5. Now decide on a job you wish to apply for from the suggestions already given and try writing the most honest letter about yourself that you can manage. The letter should be as from a school-leaver applying for a first job.

Points to remember:

— Set the letter out carefully, with your address and the date at the top right hand corner and the address of the company on the left hand side below yours. Begin 'Dear Sir or Madam'.

— Paragraph your letter carefully.
Introduction – say what position you are applying for, and how you came to know about the vacancy.

Main part – give the most important points about yourself – age, school, examinations you have taken or are studying for, when you will be available, skills, hobbies, interests, and full– or part-time work experience. Use the 'Personal Profile' checklist given in Figure 5.6.

Conclusion – say why you are specially interested in the job you are applying for. Request an interview. End with 'Yours faithfully'.

Personal profile checklist

Use this checklist each time you write a letter of application. Do not post the application until you have put a tick by *every* point.

First hurdle: Clean sheet of paper, larger than A5, unlined; straight margin, straight lines; clean and tidy appearance, no crossings out; correct spelling and grammar; clean envelope, 1st class stamp.

Second hurdle: Short and to the point; orderly presentation; relevant details about your experience and qualifications; no irrelevant personal details; no mention of previous salary; no mention why you left your last job; something to suggest you have noticed and can meet the 'hidden requirements'.

Third hurdle: An overall calm and confident impression; something to imply that you are hard-working, responsible, etc; something to make the employer think 'I must see this person to find out more'.

Spelling hints

Personnel	Advertisement	Assistant
Experience	Responsible	Opportunity
Sincerely	Appropriate	Requirements
Faithfully	Relevant	

Figure 5.6 Personal profile checklist

5.4 WHICH ONE GETS THE JOB?

Writing a letter of application for a job requires a great deal of skill. You need to be as brief as possible but nevertheless make sure that you have included all the relevant details. An example of a job advertisement follows and three letters of application for the post (Figures 5.8, 5.9 and 5.10). Read all three carefully then answer the questions at the end.

10 Beecham Croft,
Epsom,
Surrey.
S41 0HD

15th July 1992

Personnel Manager,
Rampart Ltd.,
Snowhill,
Surrey.
S22 3EQ

Dear Sir,

I wish to apply for the position of Sales Representative. I am 21 years of age and was educated at Hilltop School.

I am employed as a sales representative with Staines Ltd. I would require a salary of at least £10,000 per year. My references are P. Richards, 40 Grove Street, Moorcroft and J. L. Pierce, Longacre Road, Littletown, Surrey.

Yours faithfully,

James Smith

JAMES SMITH

Figure 5.8 Letter of application 1

75 Green Lane,
Sunnyside,
Surrey.
S43 9AD

15th July 1992

Personnel Manager,
Rampart Ltd.,
Snowhill,
Surrey.
S22 3EQ
Dear Sir,

Your advertisement for a sales representative in the 'Snowhill Echo' was just what I have been looking for. I have long admired your very successful company and would welcome the chance to work for it.

I went to school at Snowhill Comprehensive School, and I left in 1983. The teachers all seemed to like me and I always had a good school report.

My first job was with Snowhill Electronics, but their sales methods were not dynamic enough for me so I left. I am working for Peter Green now where the work is far more exciting.

I consider with my valuable experience that I should expect a reasonably high salary, but we can discuss that at the interview.

Perhaps I should have mentioned that I was picked for the Surrey under 15's football team while at school, but I felt it would take too much of my time and so I withdrew after one season.

I have chosen two very honest and well-respected members of the Snowhill community as my referees. The first is Ms N Hill, a solicitor and a J. P. Her address is, The Grange, Littletown Road, Snowhill, Surrey. The second is my uncle, Sam Smythe, a local Tory councillor who I'm sure you've seen canvassing around Snowhill town centre at the beginning of May. His address is Stoneycroft Lodge, Smallheath, Snowhill, Surrey.

I should do my utmost to please you if I got this job and I look forward with much pleasure to meeting you at the interview.

Yours faithfully,

Paul Bacon

PAUL BACON

Figure 5.9 Letter of application 2

43 Carlton Mews,
Castletown,
Surrey.
S32 0AD

15th July 1992

Personnel Manager,
Rampart Ltd.,
Snowhill,
Surrey.
S22 3EQ

Dear Sir,

I wish to apply for the post of sales representative advertised in the current issue of the 'Snowhill Echo'. I am twenty-two years of age and was educated at Littletown Comprehensive School, where I took three A levels and seven O levels, including A levels in both Mathematics and Computer Studies.

Since leaving school in 1983 I have been employed by Roberts & Co. Ltd., first as a trainee salesman, then later as a computer salesman for the south-west area. Unfortunately I feel I must leave now as there are few opportunities for promotion.

The referees I should like to offer are my sales manager and my former headmaster. Their addresses are, Pat Holt, Sales Manager, Roberts & Company Ltd., Snowhill, Surrey and Mrs P. Ryman, Littletown Comprehensive School, Littletown, Surrey.

I currently earn £8,000 per annum and I should expect a similar starting salary. However, I am aware that many companies now prefer to pay on a salary plus commission basis and I would be prepared to consider this arrangement at any interview which you care to arrange.

Yours faithfully,

Philip Timms

PHILIP TIMMS

Figure 5.10 Letter of application 3

Advertisement

Wanted – Sales Representative for newly-established computer software firm. Apply, giving details of age, education and experience, with the names and addresses of two referees to: Personnel Manager, Rampart Ltd, Snowhill, Surrey S22 3EQ.

NOW TRY THESE...

1. The advertisement asks specifically for four items of information. Which of the writers has completely ignored the first of these?

2. What criticism could be made of the referees offered by James Smith?

3. Which writer has given the most useful account of his education?

4. Who has given no real estimate of the salary he expects?

5. Who is guilty of irrelevancy? Quote one example from his letter.

6. Do you consider the details given by James Smith about his experience sufficient for the purpose? If not, what other information would you have liked to see?

7. Who has marshalled his facts so badly that one piece of important information is put in as an afterthought?

8. If you had to judge on the letters alone, to which one would you give the job?

9. Write a short criticism of the other two letters.

10. Carefully, avoiding all the faults you have just been criticising, write a letter applying for the following post:

Wanted, clerk (male or female) for postal sales firm. Typing essential. Write in first instance, giving details of age, education, experience and proof of further education since leaving school, together with the names and address of two referees to Personnel Officer, Branda Ltd, Dunmouth, Cumberland.

11. You have seen an advertisement for a junior programmer with a local computing firm. The advertisement states that a written application should be made to the personnel manager, but gives no indication of what form your application should take.

  a) State, with reasons, the format or layout which you would consider to be most suitable for such an application.

  b) Write an application which you consider will be most effective. You may invent any necessary details.

12. An advertisement in a local newspaper offers a post as a trainee programmer but gives few details and asks for applications to be made to the Personnel Manager of the company. You do not know anything about the firm but you are seeking just such a job.

a) What would you do to try to find out more about the post or the company?

b) WRITE a suitable application.

NOTE: You should choose the format or layout which seems to you to be the most suitable and, for this task, invent any necessary details.

6 Interviewing and being interviewed

OBJECTIVES

When you have worked through this chapter, you will be able to:

- list some questions you need to consider about a job, conditions of service, and yourself
- list some points to bear in mind before an interview
- list some aspects of an interview from the employer's point of view
- list some points to bear in mind when you interview someone else
- outline a form an interviewer could use to note aspects of a candidate.

INTRODUCTION

If you understand and accept the various ideas put forward in the last chapter, your chances of reaching an interview are much higher. (Unless all the other candidates have read this book too!) The interview itself is a special kind of face to face meeting where oral (speaking) skills are of great importance. That applies just as much to the interviewers as to the person on the other side of the table – so we explore both aspects in this chapter.

PREPARATION

The job

What type of skill is required?

What are the normal working hours?

Where will you normally be working?

Will you need training?

Will your workmates be your own age or much older?

Questions to ask

Decide what is most important to you in a job:

Is length of holiday important?

Is freedom of choice important?

Do you need quiet surroundings?

Do you want the chance to earn overtime or extra pay – for instance shift allowance?

Are a canteen, sports centre or other facilities important?

Know yourself

Think about what you are really like:

What are you good at?

What *don't* you like doing?

What are your hobbies and interests?

How do you compare with the person the employer is asking for?

6.1 THE INTERVIEW

An interview is a two-way exchange. You are looking for a job, and the employer is looking for someone to fill a vacancy. Neither of you is doing the other a favour. Some interviewers have training and experience in interviewing but you may well find yourself being interviewed by someone who is as inexperienced at interviewing as you are at being interviewed. You will then have to help each other.

An interview is a highly unnatural kind of meeting. You might as well recognise this, and present yourself for it in an unnaturally clean and conventionally dressed state. You may well see computer operators dressed in jeans and casual shirts, but, if you arrive dressed like that, you will immediately lose points with the interviewer. You may normally sit down in any company, or light up a cigarette, without being asked, but not in an interview. Do not arrive chewing gum, and try to avoid off-putting habits such as picking your nose.

If your letter of application or application form has done its job properly, the interviewer already has a lot of factual information about you, about what you have done and about what you enjoy doing; what he needs to discover at the interview is what sort of person you are. He can only do this if you are prepared to talk about yourself. If you have taken advantage of the opportunity presented by the letter of application or application form, the direction of the questions put by the interviewer will be those aspects of yourself, and of your activities, that you will enjoy talking about, and about which you can talk knowledgeably and intelligently. So many people fail at an interview because the two parties fail to discover any common ground, and so the interview becomes a series of mutually boring interchanges. Make sure, then, that whatever you have entered earlier about your achievements and interests, you can proceed to give a good account of at the actual interview. If you can start talking about something that really interests you, the real you can then become apparent, in spite of the artificial situation you find yourself in.

Interviewers are trained to ask questions which cannot be answered by a simple yes or no. This form of questioning is a deliberate effort to get the interviewee talking. However, if your interviewer betrays a lack of training by asking questions which could be answered by a simple yes or no, you can take the initiative by saying something like 'usually, but ...' or 'yes, unless ...', or even 'it depends what you mean by ...' An interviewer will usually ask you, probably towards the end of the interview, whether there are any questions *you* want to ask. This is your opportunity to show what a keen, critical mind you have, but you would have to be very bright to produce intelligent questions at that moment. Do ask about the firm, its products, customers and systems, and about the prospects for promotion, travel, etc. Do not ask about holidays, discount purchases, length of lunch breaks, etc.

In the end, however capable, experienced and qualified you may be, the interviewer, if he is your prospective manager, wants to know how well you and he will get along (and, of course, you need to form an opinion of that as well). The only evidence for this is how you look and what you say; even though you may find a particular subject intensely interesting, look for a response in the face of the interviewer, and, if you see any sign of boredom there, bring what you are saying to a quick conclusion and give him a chance to change the subject to one that interests him. If you should get a really bad interviewer, who does most of the talking and bores you, if you want that job try not to show how bored you are. You will probably spend relatively little time in the company of your manager once you have the job, and to be bored for half an hour in order to get the job you want is a small price to pay.

Summing up interview technique

— Think forward to the interview at the time you make the written application.

— Arrive on time, clean and conventionally dressed.

— Wait to be asked before you sit down, or light up a cigarette. Sit upright, but not stiffly with your arms folded over-defensively.

— Take any opportunity given by the questions to talk on a subject which interests you, so long as you are sure it is not boring the interviewer.

— Prepare yourself with one or two sensible questions for use if the opportunity presents itself.

— When leaving, thank the interviewer for seeing you.

— There is no perfect recipe for getting a job, but, if you can express yourself well, both in writing and in speech, and can look and sound pleasant, your chances will be greatly increased.

6.2 THE APPOINTMENT BOARD

You may well find yourself in front of not one interviewer, but a board of anything from six to twenty people. This can be an unnerving experience if you have not prepared for it.

In order to do this you should take turns with a partner at being the interviewee and a member of the board. If you are the candidate you should have a sheaf of information about the job to help you prepare. If you are a member of the board you should receive information about the job and the role you are to play during the interview (see Figures 6.1 and 6.2). Subsequently, you should be able to view and criticise your own performance, and then if time permits, try again, with different people in the different roles.

NOW TRY THESE...

Questions for candidates

Imagine that you have just applied for a job that you are interested in. Take a look at the questions listed below, some of which you may be asked when you go for an interview. Prepare yourself for the interview by writing some answers to these questions.

Which subjects did you like best at school? ____________________

Why? ____________________

Which subject are you best at? ____________________

Why? ____________________

Do you have any special hobbies or interests? ____________________

Have you taken any public exam(s)? How well do you think you did?

____

How did you hear about this job? ____________________

Why do you want to do this particular sort of work? ____________________

What do you know about this firm? ____________________

____

Points for interviewers

1 Consider the job.

2 Consider the experience and formal qualifications required.

3 Consider the personal qualities required to carry out the job.

4 Reduce the basic qualifications to no more than four or five.

5 Discuss with other selectors.

6 Consider the application in the light of formal qualifications, experience and age of applicant.

7 Consider the application in the light of the qualities required.

8 Consider the application in order to find the 'common link' with the candidate in front of you.

9 Verify any unexplained gaps in dates.

10 Arrange to eliminate or reduce interruptions during the interview.

11 Arrange the seating so that neither interviewer nor candidate is at a disadvantage.

12 Examine your own prejudices.

13 Make it immediately clear to the candidate where he/she is to sit, deposit coat, etc.

14 Adopt a 'common link' approach or an 'off balance' approach or a mixture of the two.

15 Try to keep silent so that the candidate has the opportunity to speak.

16 Head straight into the groups of subjects you want to discuss.

17 Avoid asking any 'yes/no' questions.

18 Question the candidate with the purpose of eliciting information.

19 Try to get at the truth by indirect questioning if necessary.

20 Follow up the candidate's opinions thoroughly.

21 Avoid any tendency to 'trick' the candidate.

22 Explain the job and its terms and conditions.

23 Tell the candidate when interview results will be made known.

24 Consider evidence from the candidate's past only as pointers.

25 Add your own impressions to what you have heard.

26 Make your decision.

Figure 6.1 Points for interviewers

Interview Sheet (for use by interviewers)

Name of Candidate ______________________ Date of Interview ______________

	Excellent	Above average	Average	Below average	Poor
Physical make-up					
Attainment					
Education					
Training					
Experience					
General Intelligence					
Special Aptitudes					
Words					
Figures					
Manual dexterity					
Mechanical aptitude					
Interests					
Social					
Practical					
Active (physically)					
Artistic					
Disposition					
How well does he/she get on with other people?					
Does he/she influence them?					
Is he/she self-reliant?					
Is he/she dependable?					
Circumstances					
Early background					
Present background					
Wife/Husband					
Family					

Figure 6.2 Interview sheet for note-taking

There follows a short list of questions which you may find useful to ask at the interview. Tick the three you consider to be the most important and add any others you feel are also important.

What sort of things will I be doing in this job?

What sort of training will I receive?

What sort of hours will I have to work?

What is the rate of pay and what kinds of 'stoppages' are there?

Will I have to work evenings or weekends?

Will I need any special clothing or tools?

If I'm offered the job, can I see where I would be working?

If I do well in the job, where can it lead in terms of career development?

What sort of people will I be working with?

NOW TRY THESE...

1. You are shortly to be interviewed for a post as a computer programmer. What preparations can you make beforehand and what action can you take during the interview to ensure as far as possible a favourable impression?

2. What steps would you take to prepare yourself for a job interview? Your answer should take account of

   a) the nature of the job applied for

   b) an appraisal of your strengths and how to communicate them

   c) any other practical matters

3 You are the Personnel Manager at Associated Systems Limited. Write a letter to all Branch Managers giving them guidelines on what they should be looking for when interviewing candidates for jobs. Attach a checklist which they can copy and use for each interview. The checklist should include all aspects of a candidate's performance at an interview.

4. As a manager, you have been asked to interview three candidates for a position of trainee programmer. As all have an acceptable educational standard and the necessary paper qualifications, what other factors will you wish to investigate regarding each candidate? If all prove to be equally suitable, state with reasons how you would make your final choice. In answering, make any assumptions you wish, provided that these are clearly stated.

5. Your company will shortly be conducting interviews for a post of junior programmer.

a) Design an Interview Sheet which could be used by the interviewers.

b) Describe *four* features of a well designed form.

6. You have a job interview in the next few days.

a) You may find it useful to ask some questions at the interview.
Give three examples of questions which you would ask, with your reasons for asking them.

b) Describe four personal qualities which you think the interviewer will be looking for?

c) Describe three other things which you would do to be ready for the interview.

6.3 THE EMPLOYER'S VIEW

To give you the best possible chance of success we will now look at interviews from the employee's point of view. What do good employers look for when filling a vacancy? How do they set about increasing the chances of getting the best applicant to fill the vacant position?

The task is a simple one – to choose a person who is likely to succeed in a particular job or range of jobs. Immediately this creates some uncertainty because, whichever method or methods the employer uses, it involves predicting what is going to happen in the future and that means there can be no 100% guarantee. However, the employer that has given the matter some thought will know that certain helpful assumptions can be made.

1. It is more likely that a successful selection will be made if an employer knows what it is they are looking for.

2. The best guide to future performance is past behaviour.

Before the interview our model employer will consider the job itself, why it exists, where it exists in the organisation or business and the responsibilities and duties that are associated with it. This will lead to the preparation of the *Job Description*. A *Person Specification* can then be drawn up identifying the experience and qualifications required and the personal qualities which will be needed to carry out the job. Applications will need to be considered in the light of the qualities which have been identified.

The employer will also need to remember that he or she is only human. It is important that the employer should be aware of their own prejudices, likes and dislikes, and be able to make appropriate allowances for these when interviewing. Also, thought should be given to the setting of the interview as it is essential that there are no interruptions, for example telephones ringing or callers walking in.

Thought must also be given to the seating arrangements – the employer will know that a desk or table is a psychological barrier, as is seating of different heights. An interviewee will also need to clearly see or be told where to put a coat, umbrella, hat or briefcase. Ensure also that the interviewee is not sitting in direct sunlight.

Once the employer has the candidate in front of him or her the first part of an interview plan will be to get the candidate to talk. An icebreaker or starter question will be helpful. Some common link spotted in the application might be useful. To put the candidate at ease, the interview should start with neutral questions. The interviewer will recap on what has been said to ensure the candidate's answers have been understood. The applicant will be told about the job and questions invited. The employer will avoid overtalking, moralising, arguing or giving advice.

The employer will discreetly take a note of the facts that have been brought out at the interview. This will help to give each candidate the same chance. Subjective impressions can also be noted. These notes will be most helpful in comparing candidates after they have all been interviewed and helping the employer to make up his or her mind.

The employer should always remember that he or she is in the commanding position, so does not need to show off or try and trick the applicant. After all they *have* a job, the interview is taking place on *their* territory, *they* prepare the questions, in advance and *they* have the power to appoint or reject. By comparison the interviewee has only one advantage, that of being able to tell the employer that he or she does not want the job!

NOW TRY THIS...

This assignment aims to explore the roles of interviewer and interviewee.

The assignment scenario involves a vacancy for a principal at Welling College of Further Education. The college is situated in a quiet, old-fashioned, medium-sized town and occupies an area surrounded by rundown buildings. Three miles to the south is a secondary school with a small sixth form. The parents of students at the school are mostly professional people and there is strong support for the parents' association which has successfully raised money to finance facilities such as a new computer laboratory.

The vacancy has arisen because the outgoing principal has reached retirement age. She has held her position for the last twenty years and has recently expressed concern about the role of the college in the town. Until recently the local school has shared the post–16 education, but because of the falling birthrate there are fewer students and, increasingly, more of them are choosing to stay on at the school rather than come to the college.

The outgoing principal gave an address to staff during her final year. A copy of this document is available to applicants for the post (see below).

In order to complete this assignment you should choose to be either a candidate or a member of the appointments board. Choose a false name in both instances in order to ensure an unprejudiced assessment. You will be given details of your 'character' (see following pages for board members; and for candidates), which you may expand upon but may not change. You may make notes from the details and then hand them back to your lecturer.

Copy of principal's address

Welcome to the College. I know that there has been a great deal of pressure on staff this year because of staff cuts, and an increased burden of work especially on courses designed for the lower-ability groups. May I say that I hope to be able to announce the provision of five new appointments in the coming year which should ease some of the pressure. However, it is up to us to pull together and work as a team and not to dwell on problems or blow them up out of all proportion. Perhaps we can then steer our college through these difficult times to a better future.

Our greatest problem is in attracting the right calibre of student. As you know, Welling Comprehensive School has been steadily developing its A level work. It has had tremendous support from its parents who have just set up, amongst other facilities, a computer workroom. We do not have a strong parents' association to raise money for such facilities and this obviously puts us at a disadvantage. However, I feel that we can still attract students with our well-recognised expertise in the more traditional courses, for example the Humanities. It is on developing these subjects that I propose we should concentrate our energies in the coming year. Thank you.

Chairperson of the appointments board

I represent the County Education Authority. It is my responsibility to introduce the members of the board to the candidate, to ask him or her the opening question and at the end of the interview to ask whether he/she wishes to ask any questions of the board.

The County Education Authority would be pleased to see a younger more dynamic person take over as principal of the college. The previous principal was very keen to compete with the local school but was not prepared to consider changing her very traditional concept of education. We should, however, expect any prospective candidate to have thoroughly worked out any new initiative he or she might want to introduce.

As Chairperson of this board it is important that I make sure that every member gets a chance to ask a question and that no one member gets to ask too many questions. I aim not to offer my own opinion unless the other members of the board cannot agree.

Board member 1

I am a staff member and a member of the Board of Governors of Welling College. I am looking for a candidate who will 'sweep away the cobwebs' left by our departing principal. In my view a new principal should be able to start afresh and give staff the opportunity to change some of the more old-fashioned courses. This college has gradually grown less attractive to prospective students because it has not kept up with new initiatives in education. Students nowadays want 'high-tech' courses, not traditional subjects such as English and History. I certainly will not stay at this college for much longer if the new principal does not move with the times, and I know that many of my colleagues agree with me.

Board member 2

I am a local councillor and I run my own small printing business. I really have no definite preference about the educational views of any new principal. As a business man myself I consider the job of a principal to be primarily one of management. A college such as this one has a large teaching and administrative staff. It is important that everyone feels that their roles in the college are being considered and that they feel they are not merely 'cogs in a wheel'.

I also think that a principal should be able to market his or her product – the college – and should encourage private enterprise to take advantage of courses whose content could increase their communication skills.

I will be looking for a candidate who has had some experience in the commercial world. However, in terms of candidates' educational views, I shall defer to members of the board who have some educational expertise.

Board member 3

I am a local magistrate, headteacher of Welling Primary School and a member of the Board of Governors of Welling College. As someone in the teaching profession, I am keen to see educational standards upheld. These days there are far too many 'trendy' ideas infiltrating our educational establishments. Students need to develop good sound skills in the foundations of English and Mathematics. Universities still like to see students who are well qualified in the traditional subjects.

This college has always had a reputation for a traditional curriculum and I believe this should be continued. I shall therefore ask the candidates for their opinion of the new initiatives in teaching that we hear about all the time.

I also feel that the other members of the appointments board should pay attention to my opinions as I am the most senior teaching representative on the board.

Board member 4

This board member's character and views may be devised by the student taking part in this exercise. Read through the other board members' descriptions and then write one to describe yourself.

Candidate 1

I am the Vice-Principal of Welling College. I have held this post for the past three years. In that time I have seen an unfortunate decline in student numbers and a lowering of morale among staff. I believe the reason for this decline has been because we have not kept pace with changes in curriculum development, changes that our local comprehensive school has certainly taken full advantage of. We have insisted on offering traditional A levels when, frankly, the general trend now is to become more commercially linked.

Another reason for the college's decline is the very good parents' association at Welling Comprehensive. They have been able to expand their courses thanks to financial help from parents. We have no such fund-raising organisation and I do not believe we are the sort of institution that could easily run one as parents tend not to get so involved in further education. I believe that the local education authority should recognise this and increase our budget. If I were to become principal I should seek much more student participation in decisions about the curriculum; for far too long we have neglected the rights of our students.

Candidate 2

I am the Principal of a small London college. I am applying for this post as I would like to move away from the big city, and I would like the challenge of enhancing this college's reputation in the country. I feel that I am well qualified to build up the college's standing in the community. I have been in a very similar position in my present post: I spent the first two years there gaining development grants from the council for an overseas contract to teach English to staff in a French company based in Oxford Street and for a contract with a local employment agency to teach its staff communication skills. I also started a scheme whereby interested parents could contribute their skills voluntarily as lecturers' assistants in some of the practical classes. It is my belief that a college needs a strong person in charge, someone who will increase its financial budget and also build up its reputation for upholding good solid educational methods. If parents can see that a college can guarantee their students a place in higher education, then they will surely make every effort to support that college.

Candidate 3

This candidate's character and views may be devised by the student taking part. Read through the other candidates' descriptions and then write one to describe yourself.

7 Internal communication

OBJECTIVES

When you have worked through this chapter, you will be able to:

- outline the major problem facing communication inside an organisation (for instance, a factory or large department)
- outline the purpose of an oral or written report to management and some aspects of an effective one
- state some advantages and disadvantages of suggestion systems
- list the main areas an appraiser should explore in an appraisal interview
- note some aspects of the work of employee groups (staff councils)
- explain the nature of 'need to know'
- explain the need for corporate communication and list some aspects
- describe and compare the main media of corporate communication
- list some advantages and disadvantages of the 'grapevine' and note how best to work with it.

INTRODUCTION

Whether a business, industrial, or government office is large or small, it consists of people; and whether those who operate any enterprise are many or few, they must communicate among themselves and with others to get things done. Persons at the executive level are responsible for making decisions and initiating action. For these individuals to carry out their functions effectively, they must know what is taking place throughout the company.

However, this is much easier said than done. It is very difficult to acquire a truly accurate picture of company activities, especially in organisations where there is a good distance between the men and women working on the noisy production line and the division manager seated in the office. This distance is great not only in terms of physical space, but also in terms of social stratification and professional activities. Because of these distances and what happens to the content of a message as it travels, it is often difficult for the decision maker to know exactly what is taking place on the worker level.

Information transmitted up or down the line is often distorted unintentionally or by design. The distortions that occur may be the result of honest but inaccurate evaluations of facts and situations, the desire to impress a supervisor, a wish to avoid embarrassment, or an effort to sidestep the blame for a mistake.

7.1 UPWARD COMMUNICATION

Employees of all levels, except those in top management, must communicate in an upward direction. It is vital that they transmit information clearly, concisely, and accurately, so that it may be evaluated and analysed for the purpose of making decisions. Those in charge may use such data to learn from past mistakes, to exercise better control of current situations, and to plan for future activities.

Reports

Among the most important kinds of communication to flow upwards are reports. These, if carefully controlled in number and content, can be invaluable to the supervisor or executive. He or she will usually receive them periodically from key subordinates, who should include in their reports important information on the activities of their sections, departments, or divisions. Reports written by several different department managers will often overlap and sometimes conflict.

Indeed, it is helpful if reports from different sources within a company are in conflict, for the executive receiving them must make decisions that are based on as much knowledge as possible. The action he takes may involve huge sums of money: a production line may be opened or closed, an expensive piece of equipment purchased, a contract signed, or property acquired. The correctness of the executive's decisions depends directly on the quality of the communications he receives from his subordinates; and if the information received is conflicting or overlapping, the executive can then evaluate all aspects of a given situation before making his decision.

However, if the report is unclear, incomplete, or ambiguous, or if the writer fears to recount his own mistakes or negative situations which have arisen, the actions taken or the decisions made on the basis of the report may well turn out to be incorrect and costly.

How does a firm ensure that its reports are accurate and complete? Naturally, there are many ground rules, but the most important is to have policies of communication that permit negative as well as positive situations to be reported freely. This will encourage open and honest communication and help to create a climate in which people are not penalised for reporting errors or failure in their operations.

Reports may be of two kinds: oral and written. Oral reports can be presented in formal fashion before a group, the presentation accompanied by charts, graphs, and other visual aids. Or the oral report can be as simple as a supervisor's statement: 'We produced 700 units today.' Written reports are more varied. One author has classified them according to purpose (analytical, informative or persuasive). Another writer feels that classification by type (credit, periodic, memo, examination or progress) is more accurate as a deciding factor, while still others prefer to classify them by field (engineering, marketing, management or medicine) or area of activity (research, public, annual).

Suggestion systems

There are many other possible lines of upward communication. The alert manager utilises as many of these lines as possible, seizing every opportunity to gain information that will help him make valid and successful decisions

One of the most popular methods of transmitting information upward is the suggestion box. Many companies solicit suggestions from all workers, and a monetary reward is usually given when the idea is used. In some cases the sum offered equals approximately ten per cent of the first year's savings resulting from the suggestion.

There is value in such systems, for millions of pounds are saved as a result of employee suggestions. And the psychological value an employee receives from participating in the company's production procedure is immeasurable. However, problems can arise. Sometimes the suggestion made by a worker makes a supervisor appear inefficient or incompetent because the change has not already been instituted by the supervisor. Then there is the delicate task of telling someone that his suggestion has no merit and is not eligible for an award. Still another problem is the amount of money to be awarded.

In some instances the suggestion made may cause the routine of an entire work group to change, or may result in eliminating one member of the group because of a more efficient production procedure. This obviously results in lowered group morale, ill will, and antagonism. The gain made through the suggestion may be lost twice over as a result of worker resentment.

But with all these difficulties, the suggestion system often leads to improved production and more efficient methods. Employees, on the whole, enjoy a sense of participation, and it gives management another source of information.

Interviews

Effective communication depends on dialogue; there must be some possibility of response, or feedback. Through face-to-face interaction, management can discover employees' ideas and goals, the level of rapport which exists, their willingness to share in and work toward the company's objectives, and their feelings about their own place in the corporate scheme.

Face-to-face encounters are as useful for downward communication as for upward, of course. The point is that communication becomes two-way.

Information is frequently forwarded up to management as a result of interviews held with past, present, and prospective employees. Interviews may be held for placement, to give information, to secure ideas, for induction of new employees, for evaluation of employees, for a transfer in assignment, for promotion, to discipline employees or hear their complaints, and at the time of an employee's separation from the company. If these discussions are carried through openly and honestly, they may be very valuable. Certainly every manager should sit down with each subordinate periodically and communication on a one-to-one basis.

The following documentation may help you organise appraisal interviews or take part in them.

STAFF DEVELOPMENT AND APPRAISAL SCHEME

Manager/Interviewers notes for discussion

The purpose of a development and appraisal discussion is to give you the opportunity to discuss, with your staff, performance related issues: a work plan for the coming months.

To help you and your staff obtain most benefit from discussion you will find it helpful to prepare your thoughts in a systematic way before the interview and you may find that making notes on the following points, which are not exhaustive, will serve as a useful aide-mémoire.

1. Job details

What are the main activities?

2. Achievements

a) What has been achieved in the review period?

b) What has been done well?

c) What was not achieved?

d) What needs to be improved upon?

3. Obstacles

Are there any obstacles or 'blocks' which have hindered the post holder from accomplishing agreed tasks? If so could they be eliminated?

4. In what way do you think your performance and/or style affects the post holder's performance?
5. Other work-related issues for discussion, (for example):

   a) Strengths

   b) Responsibilities

   c) Committee Work

   d) Dealing with the public

   e) Weaknesses

   f) Priorities

   g) Relationships with colleagues

   h) Aspirations
6. **Special abilities**

   Do you feel that the post holder has any special abilities which are not fully used?
7. **Improvements**

   To secure improvements in performance and make this person's job better, what additional things might be done by:

   a) You, as their manager

   b) The post holder

   c) Anyone else
8. **Work plan**

   What do you consider to be the main tasks and priorities for the next period?
9. **Career development**

   How do you see this person's career developing? What assistance is required to meet these aims?

NOTES

The purpose and/or meaning of the nine points/questions is:

1 To clarify the post holder's job. What is their role? To whom are they responsible and for what? What are the main duties, responsibilities, priorities, standards of performance and targets?

2 To review achievements against main duties. Identify the successful and less successful aspects of the operation to begin the process and determine what needs to be done to secure improvements and what action needs to be taken to bring them about.

3 Obstacles may be in the form of a 'block' which the post holder sees as preventing them from making progress in a particular direction or a 'brake' which slows down or hampers effective performance, eg poor communication, conflicting instructions, out-dated procedures.

4 The perceptive manager will be aware that their own style and performance can help or hinder the performance of others. It is, therefore, a vital part of the development and appraisal process and will provide the manager with feedback and information.

5 Can the post holder's skill, experience and potential be utilised more fully to the benefit of the Department or Authority as a whole?

6 To provide both parties with an opportunity to discuss any other job-related activity of concern.

7 Taking all aspects into account, to agree on actions necessary to maintain or improve standards of performance. This may include clarifying aspects of respective roles, adjusting targets, counselling or coaching. Who is to take what action, and when, will need to be identified.

8 Work Plan. To identify the main areas of activity to the next review period. To determine priorities for future action.

9 Career Development. To examine career aspirations and how staff see their careers developing. To discuss ways in which such development may be assisted and if appropriate to consider what training/ development recommendations might be made.

STAFF DEVELOPMENT AND APPRAISAL SCHEME

Post holder's preparation for discussion

The purpose of a development and appraisal discussion is to give you the opportunity to discuss with your manager performance-related issues; a work plan for the coming months and how your development may be furthered.

To help you and your manager obtain most benefit from discussion you will find it helpful to prepare your thoughts in a systematic way before the interview and you may find that making notes on the following points, which are not exhaustive, will serve as a useful aide-mémoire.

1. Job description

What do you consider your main activities or key task areas?

2. The achievements

a) What have you done best or with the greatest satisfaction in the review period?

b) What have you done least well or with least satisfaction?

c) What has not been achieved?

d) What needs to be improved upon?

3. **Obstacles**

   Are there any obstacles or 'blocks' which have hindered you from accomplishing what you wish? If so, could they be eliminated?

4. In what way do you think your manager's performance and/or style affects your own performance?

ACTION PLAN

This sheet should be used to identify and record areas of development in the coming year. It is likely these areas will include:

a) Personal development

b) Job development

c) Key task areas

a)

b)

c)

Signed..........................

....

Employee groups

In the last few years, especially good results have been achieved with employee groups or councils. It is exceptionally well suited to securing two-way communication between management and the work force, it results in employee recognition, and it establishes a climate for open communication.

In most firms an employee representative is elected from each department or unit. These individuals meet with management representatives on a periodic basis. One of the ground rules is that topics which may be covered by union negotiation, such as fringe benefits, grievances, or work/compensation rules, are not reviewed. All other areas are open to discussion, from 'Why is the soup in the cafeteria always cold?' to 'Why can't the units be ordered in 30-kilo instead of 60-kilo units? Handling would be much easier and safer.' A second ground rule is that answers to all questions or requests must be given at the meeting or taken up first at the subsequent conference. And still another worthwhile practice is to have minutes kept so that each item brought up is noted, as well as its disposition. These can then be distributed factory wide.

Because a group or council member is elected, he is not usually reluctant to bring up sensitive issues. He is not speaking for himself but on behalf of his work group.

Of course there must be a clear understanding that management will listen even though it may not agree to approve a change. But because most people are intelligent and fair, that is usually no problem. Employees are reasonable, and if they are listened to they will usually understand a logical refusal as easily as they will an acceptance. Subject matter seems to change after the first two or three meetings. In the initial meetings, the employee representatives have voiced almost all their real or imaginary 'gripes'. By the fourth meeting, they are suggesting methods and techniques for improving production, assembly, plant layout, etc. Certainly they are as keen on their company's success as is the management.

7.2 DOWNWARD COMMUNICATION

People work better when they know exactly what their supervisors want of them, what their duties, responsibilities, and privileges are. People need to know what is expected of them – perhaps not in minute detail, but certainly in general terms. For this reason management and supervisors must issue directives, and policy and procedural statements, to those in lower positions.

How much does an employee need to know? The answer rests in the perception of the supervisor and the needs of the employee. Some employees react strongly and unfavourably when their desires for information go unfulfilled. Others are quite passive. On the whole, however, most people want to know and to participate, not only in company production, but also in planning, goal setting, and recruiting. Of course, the employee's assignment may limit the level of 'need to know'. The press operator who repeats the same operation hour after hour, on 100mm × 100mm squares of metal sheet may have a different level of need from the engineer working on long-range corporate planning of computer needs.

Employees have a 'need to know' in two broad areas. The first is the job itself. Every employee want to know what his or her task is, how it is to be performed, how it interrelates with other tasks to achieve the company's goals and where and when it is to be performed. Employees want to know what their duties are and what freedom they have.

The second area concerns the employees' relationship with the company, the community, and their families. They want to know what management thinks about the union's demands, how management reacts to equal-employment laws, where the new plant will be built, and what are the company's goals and objectives.

The first of these two areas is easily satisfied. Printed job descriptions and on-the-job demonstration and consultation, if done conscientiously, will inform employees of the nature of their jobs. In addition, the supervisor should strive to create the kind of atmosphere in which the employees have no qualms about asking questions or requesting further explanations.

Policies of communication

Downward communication in the main is not simple. Management, when considering issues of basic interest to employees – such as strikes, benefits and redundancies – sometimes takes the view that 'if we ignore it, maybe it'll go away.' But it will not go away. If rumours are circulating, the company will suffer. Rumour leads to uncertainty, and uncertainty to fear, and fear to inability to function efficiently. For a company to continue to function successfully, there must be mutual trust, loyalty, and interest between management and employees.

The average employee is interested in vital issues such as company goals, objectives, controversies, and sensitive issues. When the company discusses these areas, it is, in essence, saying to the employee, 'We recognise you as an individual and a critical factor in the firm. Therefore we want to share important news with you that concerns the company, and therefore concerns you.' But how do you get all members of management to do this – to share, to discuss, to communicate? Some may and some may not. The objective, however, is to secure a consistent policy in all divisions, in all branches, in all locations of the company.

The answer is relatively simple, and that is to establish company-wide policies of communication. Just as a firm has policies for finance, for personnel, for marketing, for sales, for expansion ... so too should it have policies for communication.

Requirement for successful corporate policies of communication

To achieve long-range success, several corporate requirements must be stated and followed:

1. That the principle of open, honest internal communication be announced and supported by the top executive with the assurance that such communication is a vital facet of good management.

2. That employees be informed of company goals, objectives, plans and directions. This should be done in company publications, at departmental meetings, and in the one-to-one boss-worker interview.

3. That employees be informed about ongoing company activities. This should be done as quickly after the event as possible. The company newspaper, public address system, or specially convened employee meetings should be used. Nothing irritates an employee more than learning from his neighbour or a televison commentator about some activity, problem, or event in which his firm is involved.

4. That employees be informed of controversial, sensitive, and negative issues. Such issues should include recruitment problems, a drop in sales or production, cutbacks in personnel, cancellation of contracts, court actions, a decline in profits, etc.
5. That all managers actively support the communication policies. Managers must do this in practice as well as in theory. They must also understand that it isn't a matter of choice; it's an obligation they must carry through.
6. That management learn to listen and to encourage a constant flow of honest, upward communication. That it makes a real effort to listen for facts and feelings.
7. That management recognise the average employee's desire to assist his or her company in the achievement of corporate goals.
8. That management recognise that good communications must be planned, organised, and carried through with the help of professional communicators. And that it is desirable to have one person in charge of internal and external communication practices. This person can see to it that communication policies are followed in a consistent fashion in all parts of the corporation, in all printed communications, and, hopefully, in all employee relations. Such a 'communications manager' can bring the same consistency to his area as the personnel manager, the financial manager, and the marketing manager do to theirs.
9. That management support its policy with funds, time and personnel.

Of course, a policy of communication does not mean that everything must be communicated to everyone. Obviously there are constraints, boundaries, and limits. National and company security must be considered, as must competition, employee moral, and the marketplace.

Once a communications policy has been structured, stated and practised by top management, the employees' sense of security, fair play, openness, and credibility will rise as will their commitment to their jobs and their company.

Downward communication media – putting policies into practice

Effective, useful, and worthwhile communication may be achieved through several media: magazines, induction manuals, employee handbooks, annual reports, letters, video films and bulletin boards. If they are used imaginatively and creatively, they can produce results far greater than the time and materials expended on them.

Company magazines

Because the number of company magazines has grown so dramatically in recent years, it is hazardous even to guess how many are published and distributed today. However, it is safe to assume that almost every firm with more than a few hundred employees issues one periodically. They range all the way from slick, sophisticated magazines printed on first-grade paper to eight-page photocopied affairs hastily stapled together. Most of them are published under the guidance of a company editor whose primary responsibility is the magazine. Many companies use agencies which may be part of an advertising firm, or oganisations which specialise in handling company magazines.

The house magazine of today seems to fall into one of three types:

1. The most popular is the magazine that runs several feature articles on the industry of which the company is a part, the latest speech of the company president, and a story on government affairs; a fair percentage of the issue is devoted to employee activities, including weddings, births, retirements, holidays, sports, deaths, awards, and educational activities.
2. A second type is the tabloid, which may concentrate on company news, is written in a rather breezy style, and may very well have an employees' classified advertisements section.
3. The journal type of company magazine usually carries several articles of a broad, general nature. There is no news of employees or discussion of the day-to-day activities of the company. An attempt is made to publish only material of a fairly high level.

There is a definite trend in company magazines to deal with more substantial topics than was the case ten years ago. Recruitment problems, government spending, politics, cost of living, and other areas of common interest are being treated in many publications. It is true that the treatment is cautious, but at least these topics are being discussed.

There is probably no medium that can better carry company information than the thousands of company magazines published today. They can and should be used for informing employees in important areas and improving good will and understanding between employer and employee.

Company induction manuals

The policies of most companies today are so complex, their fringe benefit programs so detailed, and their rules and regulations so varied that a printed guide to them is necessary. It is virtually impossible for a new employee to learn all he needs to know about a company in a half-hour discussion with his supervisor.

It is important for both the employer and the employees to have the details available for easy and ready reference. A small company induction manual, carefully organised and clearly written, should contain the answers to most of the questions every employee has from time to time.

The value of such a manual is obvious. In the first place, it is a time saver for the employee. Secondly, everyone receives the same answer to the same question, instead of having it explained differently by different supervisors. Thirdly, and perhaps most important, the employee manual eliminates incorrect answers. Too often a worker checks with other employees or immediate supervisors. If the question is difficult and the people who answer are depending on their memories and 25 years' experience with the firm, the information given may well be inaccurate.

A typical organisation plan for an induction manual might include company history and goals, a detailed section on employee benefits, and a careful discussion of corporate policies and practices.

It is a good idea to use a spiral binder or loose-leaf notebook for the employee manual. Then, whenever a change takes place in regulations etc., it is not necessary to destroy all copies already printed. It is a simple task to reprint the page concerned with new information and substitute it for the outdated page.

The writing level and layout of the induction manual should be checked very carefully. The writing style should be concise and easy to understand. Sentences should be short and words carefully chosen.

Section dividers and topic headings should be generously used. Pictures, sketches, and completed sample forms should be added where they will do the most good.

Annual reports to employees

Several years ago quite a few of the larger corporations issued annual reports specifically for employees. These give the worker an overall view of his company's activities in the preceding year, a listing of corporate goals and objectives, some mention of new processes and developments, listings of income and expenditure, and changes in personnel.

Letters to employees

Management has used letters for years in communicating orders, claims, adjustments, etc, to customers and clients. Thousands are used in direct mail sales appeals, also dozens of different form letters to a wide variety of recipients. But it is only recently that business has learned the tremendous value of well-written letters sent to employees.

Perhaps the primary value of the letter is the personal touch it conveys. It is addressed to the employee, delivered to his home, and probably read carefully in an atmosphere that is less hurried and noisy than the factory, shop or office. The content of the letter may well be discussed at the supper table, and thus the family is drawn into company activities and interests. What better way to build company loyalty than to involve the employee's family?

Letters have other advantages as well, not the least of which are their low cost and the speed with which they can be written, reproduced, and mailed.

Topics for letters

Letters can cover a wide variety of topics very effectively. They can be used to welcome new employees; discuss a safety programme; explain new products; announce mergers, expansions, or acquisitions; examine recruitment problems; discuss company profits; or simply build good will through a sincere expression of appreciation for a job well done.

Tone

Perhaps there is no aspect of a letter that contributes more to its acceptance or rejection than its tone. The letter that sounds insincere or ingratiating, pompous or dictatorial is surely doomed to failure. Because letters usually come from the top administrative officers, they are likely to be received by the employee with some scepticism in any case. If they then live up to his somewhat cynical expectations, management would have been better off never to have sent those letters at all.

Pay envelope inserts

The message printed on a small card or slip of paper and attached to the employee's pay check is sure to receive attention. A brief announcement, a news bulletin, or a vital piece of company information can be effectively transmitted in this way.

The message should be brief and its subject matter of importance. The pay envelope insert should only be used occasionally. If every pay check is accompanied by an insert, and the topics covered are routine, the value of this special little message is soon lost.

Notice or bulletin boards

In most companies, bulletin boards are used for motivational announcements (safety, quality programmes, etc) and for announcements of broad general interest such as approaching holidays, scheduled meetings, shift changes, and recognition of outstanding employees. If bulletin boards are strategically located and carefully handled, they can be an extremely valuable device for employee communication and team building between management and the work force. When representatives of the employee group share responsibility with management for the maintenance of bulletin boards, this medium of communication can be a strong force in the participatory process of management.

First of all, bulletin boards must be well lighted and carefully placed throughout the plant. Effective positions can be found in company cafeterias (within easy reading distance of the waiting line), in changing rooms and employee washing areas, next to elevators or lifts, in employee lounges, near the time clocks, and next to the vending machines.

The boards must be kept up-to-date. It is irritating to read the same announcement every day for months. Every message should be clean, current, and attractively mounted. Sometimes coloured paper can be used as a frame or as background for an important announcement.

Some large firms use two types of boards. One of these is for the display of routine company information and employee announcements such as meetings of social clubs, and retirement parties. At times a section is also made available for a 'classified' section listing personal items for sale or being sought. The other set of bulletin boards may have glass doors with or without a lock. On this board are official company announcements. This may involve listing new corporate policies, practices, or regulations, as well as official recognition or commendation of outstanding employees.

Another way to handle this is to use one set of boards informally divided with clearly lettered headings: 'News and Views' and 'Official Company Announcements.' Bulletin boards are among the least expensive of all company communication devices and, if properly handled, one of the most effective.

7.3 LATERAL COMMUNICATION

'If someone had just bothered to tell us what was going on, we would have saved two weeks' time.'

This comment, or variations of it, is not unusual in industry today. And as organisations grow bigger and more complex, it becomes more necessary than ever for management to maintain control and have knowledge of what is taking place in various divisions, sections, and departments. As individuals become increasingly specialised, they have difficulty communicating with and understanding the ideas of other specialists.

Keeping individuals and departments, on the same level of activity, informed is lateral (sideways) communication; it is primarily the responsibility of management. This responsibility can be carried through quite easily when policies of communication have been established.

When individuals are not aware of what is taking place in a related department, unnecessary duplication of activity may result in needless expenditure of money; but money is also wasted when reports of activities are circulated to persons not concerned with the projects in question.

Here, then, strict control must be exercised. Management must decide:

— who is to be informed of which department's activities

— the amount of detail to be contained in such reporting

— the medium to be used for such communication.

Management must also understand why department heads are often reluctant to communicate their activities to other department heads. The successful manager proves to all department heads how each will benefit from good inter-company communications and thus motivates them to carry the activity through. He or she can do this by calling the supervisors together periodically and building a climate of total participation and cooperation to achieve the goals that the entire group has selected. People appreciate knowing what is being achieved in related departments. And this knowledge can often result in suggestions which lead to more efficient production, greater economies, and better use of manpower.

'The grapevine'

There is another medium of communication that exists in every organisation of whatever size or structure: the 'grapevine' (in other words, gossip). It is informal, follows no set patterns of content or direction, moves in various communication networks, and comes from the informal or social organisation among employees.

Most managers assume that the information flowing along the grapevine hardly reflects credit on the company, is often inaccurate, and not infrequently causes problems. These assumptions are often correct. But to ignore the grapevine, hope it will go away, or pretend it does not exist is hardly a solution. The grapevine does exist; it does carry information; and it can be used with benefit.

The 'grapevine', if tapped wisely, can be an excellent source of information. It can tell management what activities certain individuals or groups are engaged in, what their future plans are, and how they feel about company conditions and goals.

Some of the information in the 'grapevine' is accurate and some is not. The wise manager sifts it all and, if he is perceptive and listens carefully, he can often discover situations that are potentially troublesome. Once they are recognised, these can be discussed either with individuals or with employee groups, and the situations clarified.

The grapevine also allows people to 'let off steam.' Employees cannot usually talk back to their superiors, and some of them feel better when they can talk over their problems with others rather than bottling them up. For the person who has a strong need for recognition, the grapevine serves a useful purpose. This person can be the conveyor of news of 'major' importance.

The sensitive manager tries to tune in to the various grapevines existing simultaneously. But he also knows that what these rumours say may not be what they mean. The strong rumour that a factory is going to close down is merely a way of asking for an answer to why so many machines are being moved out.

In almost every situation, it is unwise to ignore the grapevine. Everything in a company environment will be discussed. If management does not communicate, or does not communicate accurate information about the situation, employees will communicate what best serves their purposes or what they imagine to be the case. But silence will not exist; something will flow and management is wise to let the truth circulate rather than inaccurate and harmful rumours.

One method of working with the grapevine is to identify the 'influentials' in the informal organisation of the company. These individuals strongly influence the thought and actions of fellow workers. Management should talk through problems with them, asking for their suggestions and making sure these employees understand contemplated changes or new directions in the firm.

The grapevine can also be handled through an employee council. Here representatives of various departments are encouraged to ask management about the accuracy of any rumours. Many companies also have 'question boxes' located around the plant. Employees are encouraged to drop questions in the boxes; a copy of the question and the company's reply are then posted on the bulletin boards.

Another method is the regular column in the company newspaper or magazine, which lists answers to the rumours heard on the grapevine. The questions have either been heard by management or have been sent to the editor by an employee.

Regardless of how the grapevine is handled, the important thing is to do something about it. Ignoring the messages will not cause them to disappear. The grapevine is a normal and expected method of communication in the informal organisation of a company.

Management must listen to rumours with sensitivity and perceptiveness. Careful analysis of what is said can tell management what is really going on and why a rumour is being circulated. Not only is constructive use of the grapevine possible, but it is a necessary method for securing feedback from employees in any number of areas.

Management and supervisory bulletins

Many firms issue a variety of bulletins to their different management and supervisory personnel. In some companies a system has been devised for using different colours of paper for different levels and even different divisions. It is easy to see that this system can easily get out of hand.

Some employees' jobs require that they see bulletins from several different departments and perhaps from more than one level. The result is that so many announcements cross their desks that soon they read none.

However, these are extreme situations which do not occur too often. A carefully controlled system of bulletins can prove to be an excellent way of announcing changes in policy, revisions of procedures, or information that is somewhat confidential.

Many firms feel that policies and procedures should always be communicated to employees by their immediate supervisors rather than via company announcement. In such cases, bulletins can be very effective in transmitting exactly the same information to all managers and supervisors. It is then their responsibility to communicate such information down. This obviously builds a closer relationship between supervisor and subordinate. It also strengthens the supervisor's authority, as it emphasises his position as a source of official information.

Here, as in the case of bulletin boards, control is important. Bulletins or management letters should originate only from persons who occupy specific positions. They should be written carefully and edited thoroughly. Because they often change or amend company policy, they should be numbered so that a file of them can easily be retained by the originator and the receiver.

Effective communication

Each of the above media can be used successfully in a company of almost any size. Downward communication is vitally important; management must use the media creatively and wisely, but it must have policies of communication which are consistently followed. And of major importance – management must provide channels for upward communication. Once established, management must listen to what comes up, so it will then be able to send communications down with some degree of confidence that they will be understood and (hopefully) accepted by the employees.

Internal communication

Every well-run organisation must have a carefully supervised internal communication system. Such a system must be based on a corporate policy which not only encourages two-way communication, but makes every effort to see to it that such lines exist. These lines must carry honest information in a timely fashion, up, down, and laterally. Where this system exists, the management functions of planning, organising, directing, co-ordinating and controlling are greatly assisted.

NOW TRY THESE...

1. 'Every member of management must understand that effective communication is an essential tool of good management; and that part of his or her job is to relay and interpret appropriate information and news, whether good or bad, to his or her subordinates and supporters. There is a need to inform employees about matters which affect them or their jobs, to interpret management's position on relevant issues ...'

Lyn Townsend, former
Chairman of the Chrysler
Corporation.

Identify _four_ different methods for communicating information downwards in an organisation and describe their relative advantages and disadvantages in detail.

2. A manager is proposing to move a department of a business to another location. What forms of communication should (s) he use to consult (and persuade) the employee(s) about the plan and to put the intended move into operation. Also discuss other possible methods and the reasons for their rejection.

OR

A merger between the small firm which you manage and a much larger group of companies has been decided. The news will shortly be published in the press. How and when should you inform your employees of the change? What details will it be necessary for you to communicate?

3. You are a Personal Assistant to Mr Brighton, the Managing Director of a large canning factory on a new trading estate. The complex comprises a works unit, in which 400 workers are employed, an office unit with 100 Sales and Office staff and a holding warehouse with 25 staff.

All the units are linked by tannoy, telephone and have internal mail deliveries three times a day. Apart from the workers' clock cards, in which messages can be left, there are general and specific notice boards throughout the complex with a large general board in the canteen.

The following messages need to be relayed. From the methods available choose which you would use to: -

a) Inform the Personnel Manager that the 1430 meeting with the Managing Director has been cancelled.

b) Inform the staff that the company bus timetable has changed and that buses will now leave the main site at 1725.

c) Inform Robert Smith a temporary casual worker that he is to be given an apprenticeship.

d) Inform the staff that the canteen is being left in a disgusting condition and that the canteen staff are very annoyed with the situation.

e) Inform the members of the Associated Canning Union that there will be a Branch Meeting at 1700 in the Work's canteen.

YOU MAY USE MORE THAN ONE METHOD

Explain why you have chosen these methods and what factors you have taken into consideration.

4. a) Define the term 'communication' as it applies in business and industry.

   b) Taking examples from a typical work situation illustrate: -

      (i) The importance of communicating
      (ii) Types of communication, eg telephone calls
      (iii) Methods of communication

5. Examine four problems of communication in business. In what ways can these situations be improved.

6. There is about to be a major reorganisation of your workplace, which will include the relocation of staff and resources within the same building, the breaking up and reformation of work teams, and the introduction of labour saving technology.

a) Draw up a step-by-step guide that could be adopted by your management team. This should offer advice on the best way to communicate their proposals to the staff.

b) Draw up a list of six subjects that you believe will worry staff most of all.

7. Identify *four* methods for communicating information downwards in an organisation and describe their relative advantages and disadvantages in detail.

8. a) Your company will be conducting an interview for the post of junior systems analyst. Design an Interview sheet which could be used by the interviewers.

   b) Describe *four* features of a well designed form.

8 Effective meetings

OBJECTIVES

When you have worked through this chapter, you will be able to:

- — list some functions of small group meetings
- — list some administrative aspects of planning a meeting
- — list the main tasks of the person chairing the meeting during the planning stage
- — describe the main tasks of the person chairing the meeting in progress
- — outline some of the ways in which effective and ineffective meeting groups differ
- — list the main skills of a good chairperson.

INTRODUCTION

Business meetings can vary in their type, purpose, scope, size, content and style. They can range from the large, formal gathering where rules and procedures are closely defined and strictly followed, to the small, informal meeting between two or three people who have got together to discuss some common interest. Most day-to-day business meetings tend towards the informal type. Some form of control is obviously necessary, but the over-use of procedures and formality will often stifle, or at least restrict, free thought and discussion.

We are concerned here with the normal business meeting, whose effectiveness (or otherwise) can be measured in terms of the quality, clarity, economy and relevance of its discussion and result, and the speed with which questions are resolved and action taken. We are not so much concerned with formal gatherings where rules and procedures tend to carry a disproportionate importance, and where the opportunity to voice opinions, put forward motions, pass resolutions and vote on issues is an essential part of the proceedings.

As with other forms of communication, meetings will be effective only when:

- — there has been proper preparation;

— the aim is clear and understood by everyone;

— the possible existence of barriers has been recognised and plans made to overcome them;

— content is relevant;

— communication takes place in an ordered manner;

— checks are made to see if the aim is being/has been achieved;

— those involved possess and use the necessary skills.

8.1 PREPARATION

There are two aspects to preparing for a meeting (see Figure 8.1): making the administrative arrangements, and preparing for the conduct of the meeting itself. The administrative arrangements will cover such things as choosing the right people to attend and selecting a convenient date, time and place; sending out the convening instructions, particularly details on the aim of the meeting and its agenda and any background material that may be necessary; arranging for seating, place cards, stationery, secretarial support, telephones, refreshments, reception, etc. The extent to which these various arrangements are necessary will of course depend on the size, formality and complexity of the meeting.

- Administration
- Information
- Purpose (chair)
- Resources (chair)
- Anticipate (chair)
- Planning (chair)
- Relevance (all)
- Ordering (chair)
- Monitoring (chair)
- Skills (all)

Figure 8.1 Preparing for a meeting

Although all of these points carry some importance (particularly those concerned with circulating the aim and agenda) many of them are nothing like as essential to the conduct of an effective meeting as is sometimes thought. It is perfectly possible to conduct an effective meeting on an *ad hoc* basis and even in disagreeable physical circumstances, provided there has been adequate preparation for the conduct of the meeting itself!

Whoever is going to chair the meeting must obviously prepare for it, and if it is to be effective, so must each member. It is essential that the Chairman comes to the meeting with a very clear idea of the purpose of the meeting, his aim, and how he intends to achieve it. None of this implies a rigid, authoritarian approach – the plan must always be flexible and responsive to the particular characteristics of the meeting. There must, however, be some kind of plan. Just as one would not think of setting off on a journey without a clear idea of destination, route, methods of transport, obstacles, etc, so a Chairman should not convene a meeting without equally careful thought and planning. To achieve a successful plan, the following points should be observed:

— Be quite clear as to the purpose of the meeting

— Meetings can be called for various reasons, and the type of meeting will often influence its conduct.

— Decide on the main aim. This should be done as precisely as possible, and limits established. The aim should be capable of being expressed in such a way that it is perfectly understood by everyone present at the meeting; the goal to be reached by the meeting should be clearly defined and progress towards achieving that aim should be measured.

— The Chairman should also consider the resources he will have available, ie the knowledge and skills of the various members; how he can best use these resources.

— Try to anticipate any likely obstacles and difficulties; consider how they might be overcome.

— Develop a plan for getting the meeting from its starting point to its desired goal as effectively as possible, and make sure the discussion does not stray too far away from the relevant subject.

— Each member should be informed of and think about the purpose and aim of the meeting in advance. This will help to get a common understanding of the task established as quickly as possible.

— Anticipate the possible course of discussion.

— Gather information and references.

— Decide which topics or points should be raised and prepare a plan to have these views and opinions put across.

— Anticipate any reactions and objections, and plan to counter them.

Although not a conscious part of the preparation for any particular meeting, the acquisition and development of the skills needed for effective participation – whether as Chairman or member – is implicit in the overall process of 'preparation'.

8.2 CONDUCT AND STRATEGIES

The two most important requirements for effective meetings are that communication should take place in an ordered manner, and that content should be relevant. Too often it is assumed that both these are the responsibility of the Chairman, who achieves them by 'controlling' the meeting. There are obviously instances when such 'control' is necessary, but responsibility for orderly communication and relevance lies with every individual member. Both requirements can in fact be achieved without a Chairman at all – if every member adopts the self-discipline needed to achieve an effective meeting (see Figure 8.2). In some cases, control of the discussion can change hands during a meeting, resting at any point in time with the member who appears to be best qualified to deal with the particular phase the discussion has reached.

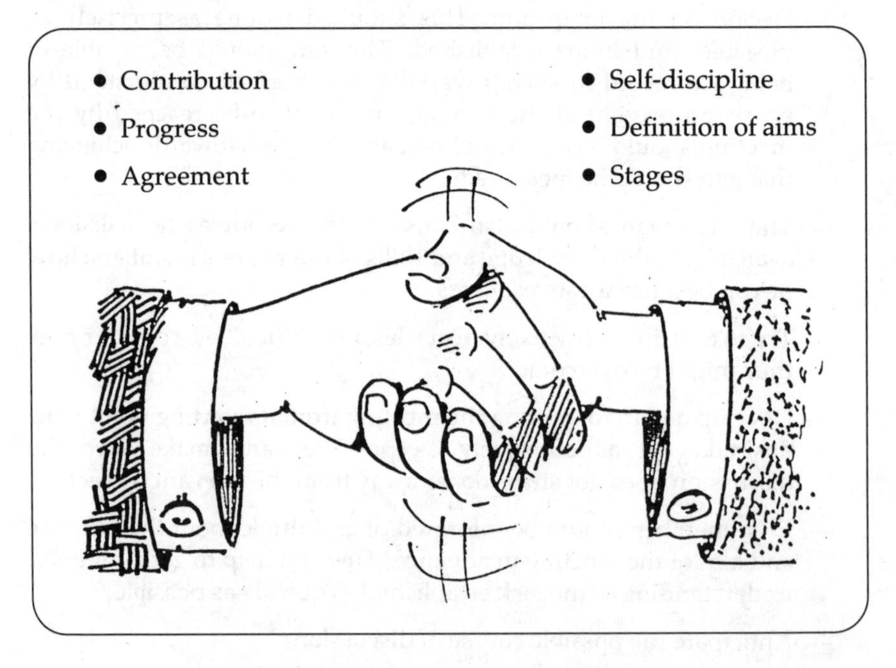

• Contribution
• Progress
• Agreement
• Self-discipline
• Definition of aims
• Stages

Figure 8.2 Conduct at a meeting

There is no instant recipe for the effective conduct of a meeting. However, some important ingredients do exist and should always be present. The aim of the meeting, for instance, must be clearly understood by all present. This aim may be defined by the Chairman, or evolved by discussion, but it must be understood and accepted by everyone present before the discussion goes any further. Its limits must be drawn clearly enough in everyone's mind for them to recognise at once when they are straying off the point. If the meeting is seeking an end product, then this too must be defined sufficient clearly for everyone to recognise either its achievement, or the extent to which it has not been achieved.

It is also helpful for the meeting to agree an outline plan for achieving its goal. For example, a complex subject can sometimes be broken down into stages. Identifying and agreeing these stages early in the meeting can help control its progress and improve the relevance of the discussion.

From time to time, progress towards the goal should be checked. This may be done by the Chairman, or by any other member of the meeting. The essential point is that there should be an opportunity for everyone to review how things are going, and to make any necessary adjustments. Everyone present must also have the opportunity to contribute his or her views. This may mean restraining some members, and encouraging others – often the most difficult task facing a Chairman, and one that requires great skills. At the end of the meeting, before members disband, its outcome and the way it has gone should be assessed. Agreement should also be reached on what action should be taken and what remains to be done.

8.3 FOLLOW-UP AND MINUTES

No meeting can be said to have been effective until any follow-up action agreed upon has been completed. Although it is important to circulate minutes as quickly as possible, details of what follow-up action is necessary should, as indicated above, be agreed before members disperse.

The writing of minutes requires considerable skill. The aim is to record the essentials without giving a blow-by-blow account of the meeting, yet not leaving out anything important. Unless the meeting wishes to have a particular point of view stated in full and its author identified, it is usually sufficient to record decisions in the form 'It was agreed that ...'. Another useful tip to include an 'Action By' column on the right hand margin of each page. The appointment or name of the person required to take action is entered in this column, opposite the item concerned. This makes it much easier to see who is required to do what, and allows progress on action taken to be checked. Apart from accuracy, the most important thing about minutes is that they should be circulated as soon as possible after the meeting, whether for approval or for executive action by the members.

8.4 EFFECTIVE AND INEFFECTIVE GROUPS

- Objectives
- Relevance
- Participation/listening
- Atmosphere
- Criticism
- Conflict
- Feelings
- Decision-making
- Follow-up
- Group working

Figure 8.3 Effective and ineffective groups

A COMPARISON CHART OF EFFECTIVE AND INEFFECTIVE GROUPS

	Effective Group	Ineffective Group
Objectives	Aims and objectives clearly formulated and understood. Accepted by all members.	Objectives not clearly defined. Often conflict arises because individuals have personal private aims, or in the absence of stated aims assume them.
Relevance of discussion	Relevant discussion, with virtually everyone contributing.	Dominated by a few; matters discussed are often irrelevant.
Participation and listening	Everyone is prepared to listen to each other and consider the points made. Members should not be afraid to put forward views and ideas.	Members do not give each other a fair hearing; contributions are often irrelevant and made for effect. It is clear that some members are hesitant to state their views, fearing ridicule or condemnation.

Atmosphere	Tends to be informal and relaxed; all members of the group are involved and interested.	Formal, tense, with undercurrents of antagonism. There is obvious indifference and boredom.
Criticism	Accepted as being a constructive element and welcomed.	Often destructive and made as a result of personal antipathies.
Handling of conflict	Disagreements are not suppressed, but carefully examined, and attempts are made to resolve them. Dissenters are not dominated nor is there 'tyranny of the minority'.	Disagreements may either be completely suppressed or result in open conflict. Often a vote is taken, and a large minority are dissatisfied. A sub-group can be so aggressive that the majority give way.
Expression of personal feelings	Members feel free to express their own feelings and attitudes towards the problem.	Personal feelings are often kept hidden under the surface.
Decision making	Decisions arrived at by consensus. Individuals are not afraid to disagree and are given fair consideration. Formal voting seldom used and a simple majority is not considered a suitable basis for action.	No systematic discussion or consideration of everyone's views. Decisions arrived at without overall agreement; action often taken prematurely. Formal voting frequently used despite only a small majority.
Follow-up action	Decisions and follow-up action determined and everyone is fully aware. Jobs are allocated clearly and apppropriately.	Neither decisions nor actions are clearly defined therefore the possibility exists that tasks handed out will not be fulfilled.
Leadership	The Chairman does not dominate nor are the	Leadership may be jealously guarded by

	members subservient to him. Leadership role may shift to the appropriate person with the most knowledge and experience.	the Chairman. Alternatively, there may be a struggle for leadership in order to exert influence or achieve status.
Group working	Group aware that to operate efficiently, it must frequently review what it is doing and maintain a self-conscious attitude.	Group not prepared to acknowledge or discuss its own deficiencies.

LIMITING FACTORS

- Experience
- Knowledge
- Fear
- Behaviour
- Dominance

Figure 8.4 Limiting factors

Many of the above points may seem obvious, but experience shows that this is not necessarily so. The question therefore is 'Why?'. There appear to be a number of possible explanations:

— people's experience of really effective groups is very limited, and there are no clear standards to go by;

— few people have knowledge of the factors that distinguish effective from ineffective groups;

— fear of conflict, hidden hostilities and underlying personal factors are difficult to overcome.

Yet another inhibiting factor in the success and effectiveness of a meeting is the misapprehension that the effectiveness of a group rests solely with the leader. In fact, research indicates that it is skilful membership behaviour which is the operative factor. The greatest danger of all is that the person with the loudest voice or strongest personality will become Chairman and totally dominate the meeting, so that those who have relevant knowledge and opinions are not heard.

8.5 TYPES AND SIZES OF MEETING

Purposes

It is difficult to lay down hard and fast rules for classifying meetings and discussions. Sometimes they are confined to one category but they may also take in several categories (see Figure 8.5). It is important, however, to be quite clear about the purpose of any meeting or discussion and a list of common reasons for calling a meeting is given below.

• Give information
• Seek ideas
• Co-ordinate
• Release
• Involve
• Negotiate
• Resolve
• Policy
• Plan
• Decide
• Act

Figure 8.5 Purpose of meeting

Giving Information:

— to hear a statement of policy;

— to receive instructions, or learn about new procedures;

— to brief a group of subordinates.

Note: opportunities may be given for questions and/or discussion.

Obtaining information or ideas:

— to hear subordinates' views on a problem;

— to find out what happened;

— to investigate a situation;

— to obtain information for a report.

Note: this type of meeting does not necessarily come to any decision, but usually involves discussion.

Progressing or co-ordinating activities:

— to discuss what action is needed;

— to co-ordinate the work of different sections or departments.

Airing feelings or grievances:

— to allow people to 'let off steam', for example.

Negotiating a contract or agreement:

— with Trade Unions or a contractor, for example.

Resolving a problem:

— to clear up confusion;

— to overcome an obstacle to the implementation of a plan;

— to discover what the problem is;

— to investigate a technical difficulty.

Taking non-executive action:

— to get their support for a plan of action;

— to get their views and ideas;

— to develop their capabilities;

— to motivate them and get commitment.

Taking executive action:

— to get something done;

— to carry out a higher management plan.

Note: information may move from one person outwards, from many persons inwards or be multi-directional (see Figure 8.6).

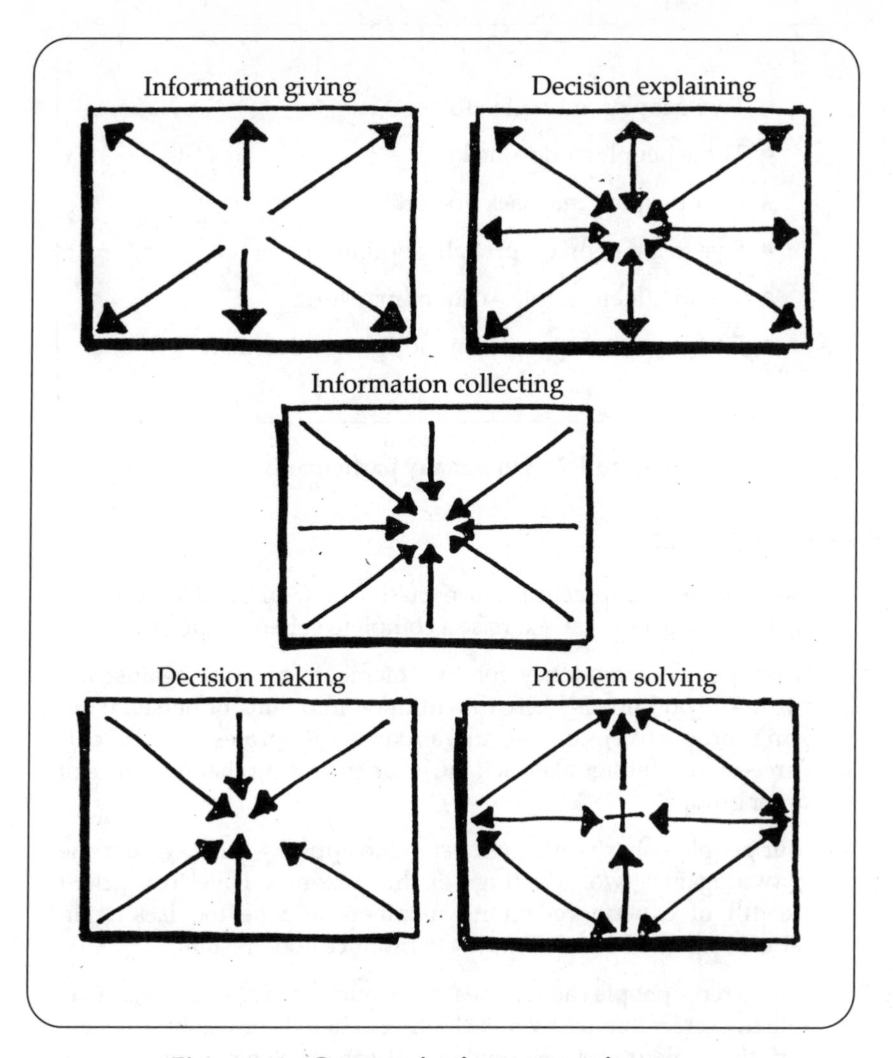

Figure 8.6 Communication patterns in groups

Formulating policy:

— about the use of certain equipment, for example.

Preparing a plan or recommendation:

— to formulate proposals for senior management to consider, for example.

Reaching a decision:

— how to apply a plan;

— what to do about something or someone.

- Two people – mutual veto
- Three people – odd-one out
- Four people – may lack breadth
- Five to ten people – probably optimum
- Ten to fifteen people – cliques may form
- Fifteen or more people – minority may dominate

Figure 8.7 How many participants

Sizes (see Figure 8.7)

— Two people – impractical since biased or freakish decisions are likely. Each person can exercise a complete veto over the other.

— Three people – tendency for two members to unite against the third. The odd one is likely to withdraw into him– or herself (stop being productive), or set up a damaging protest movement. Three-man meetings also lack the error-correcting characteristics of larger groups.

— Four people – sharp divergences tend to appear – three against one or two against two. Meetings of this size may have insufficient breadth of experience among members and be too lacking in variety and intellectual stimulus to produce good results.

— Five to ten – people can talk nearly as much as they want to and are able to exert influence over each other. There is probably sufficient variety of talent and personality to treat problems imaginatively. Good conditions for interaction and therefore for group problem-solving.

— Over ten – as the group grows in numbers an increasing number of people are scared into silence. Intimate face-to face contact becomes difficult and the group may split into cliques.

— Over fifteen – low participators stop talking to other members of the group and either stay silent or talk only to the few. Thus interaction – and creativity – freeze. Some large groups, however, can solve certain kinds of problem more effectively than similar smaller groups – eg where there is a correct and variable answer, say, the cheapest method of erecting a fence or building a cycle shed. In addition, the more people in the group the more chance there is that it contains an expert who knows the answer.

8.6 REQUISITE SKILLS

'Skill' is defined as 'the ability to do something'. In a meeting or discussion many different kinds of things have to be done to produce effective results (see Figure 8.8). For instance the aim needs to be stated; facts need to be elaborated; ideas need to be linked and related; conclusions have to be drawn. By virtue of their experience and personal characteristics, some people are better at doing some of these things than others. An effective meeting is one where these skills are recognised, and used to the benefit of all. The Chairman alone cannot be expected to be equally strong in all skills. Members must therefore use their own strengths to supplement those of the Chairman.

- Formulation-definition
- Research
- Illustration
- Clarity
- Analysis
- Leading
- Summarising
- Deducing
- Responsive
- Stimulating
- Steering
- Constructive
- Reconciling
- Listening
- Observing
- Assessing

Figure 8.8 Requisite skills for an effective meeting

Here are some examples of the skills that need to be exercised by a competent Chairman and some of the techniques involved:

Formulating aims/stating aims	Defining the aim; re-wording statements; writing down aims.
Seeking information/ seeking opinions	Asking for facts; searching out ideas; formulating relevant questions.
Giving information/ giving opinions	Offering relevant information; putting forward ideas or opinions; giving examples to stimulate discussion.
Clarifying/elaborating	Clearing up confusions; interpreting ideas or suggestions; questioning meaning; asking for elaboration of a point; clarifying purpose.
Analysing	Breaking down ideas; deciding what is relevant or significant; identifying the ingredients of a problem.

Proposing	Making firm propositions about what should be done next; leading the discussion forward.
Summarising	Linking related ideas; re-wording suggestions; putting forward intermediate conclusions; summarising progress.
Deducing/drawing conclusions	Bringing discussion to an effective conclusion; sending up 'trial balloons'; making deductions from information given.

There are also other kinds of things that need to be done mainly concerned with helping people to work together:

Creating confidence/ creating security	Putting people at ease; being warm and friendly; being responsive to people's contributions; showing regard for others.
Encouraging/stimulating	Encouraging participation; encouraging silent members' participation; helping people to use their skills; sparking off thought.
Steering	Suggesting ways in which progress might be made; re-directing the course of discussion; helping the meeting to adjust its methods of working.
Supporting	Being constructive; building and developing other people's ideas and contributions; preventing good ideas or useful facts from being lost; making your own view clear.
Reconciling	Exploring differences; emphasising similarities.
Listening	Really concentrating on what other people are saying; being less concerned with your own personal contribution; thinking, but not interrupting.
Observing	Watching what is happening and how people are reacting; noting pressures or tensions; monitoring progress towards the aim.
Reviewing/assessing	Assessing how far the aim is being achieved; identifying what is helping or hindering progress.

How do you rate as a chairperson?

Read through the following points and tick as appropriate.

1. I vary my style according to purpose of the meeting.

2. I know how to deal with 'hidden agenda' items – power struggles, jealousies, rivalries, etc – and so relieve the group's inner tensions.
3. I encourage people to bring their negative feelings out into the open by skilful questioning and careful listening.
4. I try to not to let members quarrel over mere words and generalisations. When two people disagree I ask each one to specify the factor(s) they disagree with and give examples of what they mean.
5. Sometimes I deliberately reduce my own authority in meetings in order to create a free atmosphere. I know three techniques for doing this.
6. If people wander from the problem-path I know how to call them back *with tact*.
7. I know the kind of seating arrangements which encourage interaction.
8. I help the committee to keep track of its progress by summarising the discussion from time to time and by keeping a record of promising ideas for future reference.
9. I don't overwork the committee, and give it adequate time to solve complex problems. If time is limited I shorten the agenda.
10. At the end of the meeting I summarise the ground covered, decisions made and any action to be taken and by whom.

NOW TRY THESE...

1.Meetings play a vital part in any modern organisation. What is their importance and what characteristics do effective meetings display?

2. a) Why are effective meetings so important in the running of large businesses?

b) Define the role of:

i) The Chairperson

ii) The Agenda

iii) The Minutes

3. a) As the Chairperson at a meeting, what practical preparations would you make to ensure that the meeting was a success?

b) What rules of procedure should be observed to ensure an effective meeting?

4. A works consultative committee has been set up in your firm and you are appointed secretary. Describe the correct procedure for calling a meeting, the duties of the secretary before and during the meeting and the points you would bear in mind when writing up the minutes afterwards.

5. Meetings can be an exciting and rewarding element in business life. Why then is frustration, boredom and a low level of accomplishment the outcome of many meetings.

6. Explain what you consider to be the essential requisites of good Chairpersonship.

7. a) What is the difference between a business meeting and a group of people talking things over informally?

   b) Decribe briefly four reasons why meetings are held at work.

8. Your company is to hold an exhibition of its computer equipment and software.

   a) Draw up an agenda for a meeting of the Company staff to organise the event.

   b) Describe six factors which will determine whether the meeting is successful or not?

NOW TRY THIS...

In this problem, a meeting of some staff has been called to discuss a situation that has arisen within a particular department. Four people are involved and each student is asked to assume the role of one of those present. The roles are described on different pages so that each student reads only his own role.

The background to the problem is as follows:

At the request of some members of the Department, the head has called a meeting to discuss the procedure by which senior vacancies in the Department are filled. In the past, these vacancies were advertised only internally and it seemed to be the policy to promote from within the Department rather than to bring new people from outside. Recently. however, this policy seems to have been reserved and vacancies are now advertised in the local and/or national press. Of course, it has still been open to people already working for the Department to apply but, in nearly every case, the appointment has gone to an external applicant. This change of policy has caused some comment in the Department. Many people who are hoping for promotion within the firm feel that it is unfair and it is because of the comments that have been made that this meeting has now been called.

The following are the people at the meeting:-

Head of Department

A who has been with the Department several years

B who has recently joined the Department from outside and who was appointed over the head of **A**

C who has been with the Department for two years and is known to be looking for work elsewhere.

Head of department

The following is the role of the Head of Department.

You have been concerned about the comments which have been passed within your Department relating to the Company's new policy of advertising vacancies externally, rather than filling them by internal promotion. When this change of policy was being considered at a meeting of Heads of Department, you said you felt there were strong arguments for continuing to promote internally; you felt that this was good for morale within the organisation and that there were usually people already in Departments whose ability meant that they could successfully fill senior positions. However, most Heads were in favour of bringing in 'new blood' and it was agreed as a general rule that posts would be filled from outside. That meeting took place several months ago and in the intervening period you have seen the new policy operate successfully; people appointed from outside have brought with them new ideas which have been useful to the Department. Your situation at this meeting is as follows:

1. You cannot change the new policy. You can agree to raise it for discussion at a Head's meeting but do not think this would be much use.
2. Although you were against bringing people in from outside, now you are not so sure.
3. You are very concerned at the effect which the new policy is having on morale within the Department. Somehow things must be put right!
4. You want to hear as many views as possible at the meeting. Some members of the Department such as **A**, are very vociferous, others, such as **C**, are too quiet. Your job is to maintain a balance in the contributions and to draw out the more reserved members. You want as full a discussion as possible.

Now open the meeting.

Participant A

The following is the role of **A** at the meeting.

You have worked in the Department for several years and during that time have acquired useful experience and additional qualifications. You enjoy working for this company and, as you live nearby, it is a convenient place to work. For these reasons, you have not looked for work elsewhere and have been hoping for internal promotion. When a senior position became vacant within the Department a few months ago, you expected it to be advertised internally and that you would probably be appointed. You were surprised when the post was advertised in the press and to learn subsequently that this was because there had been a management decision to advertise all senior positions in this way. You applied for the job and were interviewed but not appointed. The person appointed came from another company and, after the interview, the Personnel Manager explained that this was because a policy decision had been made to bring in 'new blood' from outside. This made you angry. What has made you even more angry is the fact that the new appointee, to whom you are now responsible, is taking quite a long time to 'learn the ropes' and that while he is learning you are effectively doing his job. Two weeks ago you went to see your Head of Department and expressed your anger. He agreed to call a Departmental meeting and at this meeting you are determined to put your views forward fully and very forcefully. You are angry and bitter and everyone is going to know how you feel! You are going to try to dominate the meeting and let **B** know what you think of him.

Participant B

The following is the role of **B** at the meeting.

You have recently joined this Company. A few months ago a senior post in this Department was advertised and you applied for the position and were subsequently appointed. You are well qualified both on paper and in terms of experience and you feel that you have new and useful ideas to bring to your new job. When you were told at your interview that it was policy to bring in 'new blood', you said you agreed with this and, in fact, believe this to be the case. However, starting with the new company has not been easy: it has taken a while to 'learn the ropes' but you think you have done this quite quickly; what has made things very difficult is that you were appointed over a person (**A**) who had been working in the Department for several years and who clearly resents you as the result. This meeting is going to be awkward for you; on the one hand, you feel the policy to bring in new people is right and want to defend it; on the other, you do not want your relationship with **A** to deteriorate further and are reluctant to appear in open conflict with him – there may be the opportunity to show the Head that you can be tactful. You want to make a good impression as someone who can be forceful yet concise and diplomatic.

Participant C

The following is the role of **C** at the meeting.

You have worked in the Department for two years. You are not very interested in the Company or in the work you are doing and have now decided to look for employment elsewhere. You have heard that the Management has made a policy decision to bring in 'new blood' rather than promote internally, but this has not affected your decision to leave as you were going to do this any way. You do not care what is decided at the meeting and your main aim is to say as little as possible in the hope that the meeting will end quickly and you can go home early. In your opinion the issue under discussion is not an important one and if people do not like where they are working they should move out, just as you intend doing. You do not like either **A** or **B** as they are both ambitious. If you say anything at all, it will be with the intention of bringing the discussion to an early close.

9 Taking sides

OBJECTIVES

When you have worked through this chapter, you will be able to:

— describe, with examples, how a written report (perhaps in a newspaper) may be biased
— describe the three main steps of preparing for a negotiation
— describe the three main steps of the actual negotiation
— explain some of the rules of negotiation.

INTRODUCTION

Taking sides is a part of normal human activity, both verbal and non-verbal. Even non-verbal activities, such as football, call forth strong verbal support for one team and abuse for the other, but here we are concerned with those activities with whose main content is verbal rather than physical.

We take sides in a discussion, a debate, an argument, a negotiation. Newspaper reporters and editors take sides in the emphasis they give to the virtues of one political party or political system, the government or the trade unions, the North or the South, the East or the West, and so on.

In this chapter, we concentrate on two aspects of taking sides verbally: negotiating, with the purpose of achieving a settlement satisfactory to both sides, and commenting, with the purpose of justifying one course of action or party, while vilifying another. We will take this latter aspect first.

9.1 SLANTED COMMENT

Emotive words

Some newspapers (the extreme minority) do their best to report objectively, giving equal weight to both sides and leaving the readers to form their own conclusions. An example, taken from *The Guardian* of 19 June 1984, is shown in Figure 9.1. Re-write this article as you would imagine it would appear in a typical left-wing, or trade union newspaper report, then re-write it as a typical right-wing newspaper report.

Accounts of Scargill injury clash

Black day for picket battle violence

By Malcolm Pithers

The worst scenes of violence in the miners' dispute broke out at the Orgreave coking plant near Rotherham, Yorkshire, yesterday with cars being burned, stones, bricks and bottles being hurled, and policemen lashing out with truncheons.

The battle lasted for 10 hours of horrific clashes. At the end 93 had been arrested and 79 injured – 51 of them pickets and 28 police officers.

Among the injured was the miners' president, Mr Arthur Scargill who was detained in Rotherham Infirmary last night for observation.

His condition was not serious and hospital staff said he was suffering from head, arm and leg injuries. He was taken to hospital amid conflicting versions of how his injuries were sustained.

Mr Scargill said he believed he was struck by a police shield from behind. The assistant chief constable of South Yorkshire, Mr Tony Clement, said he was standing only a few yards from the miners' president and saw him fall on a railway banking.

He said Mr Scargill struck himself accidentally against what looked like a railway sleeper.

Mr Clement said he could not speak for what may have happened earlier, but he saw Mr Scargill standing near two men. The miners' leader had slipped near some chain link fencing and fallen down backwards.

Mr Clement said that the miners' leader then struck the back of his head on what he, Mr Clements, thought was the sleeper.

Mr Clement — "saw miners' leader slip"

He went across to talk to Mr Scargill and found him obviously concussed. He spoke to the men nearby and told them Mr Scargill needed help. They told him that two lads would look after him, but Mr Clement insisted that Mr Scargill needed professional help as soon as possible.

Another account of what happened came from a miner, Mr Stephen Hallow from Silverwood Colliery, who said that the police charged towards them.

He said he saw Mr Scargill on the floor out of the corner of his eye. He said as far as he was concerned he had been given a 'good leathering'.

Police riot squads were used yesterday and several mounted police charges were made. Throughout the day missiles of every site and type were hurled towards police lines.

At one point the police said that two petrol bombs had been thrown. But it seemed later that these had been canisters of bottles filled with diesel fuel.

In an attempt to cool the situation magistrates ordered all pubs within two miles of the plant to stay shut at lunchtime. The order was made at the request of the South Yorkshire Chief Constable, Mr Peter Wright. Police then toured pubs and off licences ordering them to close.

Miners began converging on the Orgreave plant at 3am yesterday. Some had travelled from Scotland, Wales, the North-east of England as well as Yorkshire.

At one stage they practically overwhelmed police units. There were pitched battles inside the coking plant for the first time since picketing began, and the frustration on both sides spilled over into sickening scenes of miners being batoned and of police being attacked with bricks, slivers of glass as well as the containers of fuel.

Although the police lines eventually held, officers did react violently. Truncheons were drawn and used on individuals by snatch squads.

The day produced unreal, pitiful scenes. Cars were rolled downhill towards policemen and ignited to make a flaming barricade.

At one point I heard a policeman yell at a photographer to take photographs of a hero. He was pointing to a mounted police officer whose arm was bleeding badly. An ambulanceman was holding the wound to stem the flow of blood.

It was equally sickening to hear policemen clapping and cheering as a picket, bleeding heavily from a head wound, was helped into an ambulance. While this was happening police were being pelted with missiles.

At the height of the battle two men who run a local transport works a few hundred yards from the plant found miners battering down the doors of their works. They told Mr Ashton Whittingham and Neil Manning that the police had been filming them from his garage.

A diesel tank was then emptied and bottles and canisters filled. Vehicles inside were hauled out and used in the barricade.

Earlier in the day I had walked with miners converging on the plant near this garage. At that time there was a peaceful mood.

Later I returned to the same spot to find the barricade across the road. A few yards further on wooden stakes had been placed in lines to prevent any police horse charges.

The barrage of rocks, bricks and glass was kept up for hours. For most of this time policemen stood with riot shields to fend off the missiles. Charges were also made against the pickets with policemen lashing out with truncheons.

Mr Clement who is in charge of the Orgreave operation, said later that it was a miracle no one had been killed. What people had witnessed could only be called a riot.

Figure 9.1 Excerpt from *The Guardian*, 19 June 1984

Two expressions which occur frequently in newspaper reports are 'terrorist' and 'freedom fighter'. Can you think of other pairs of words which biased reporting might employ to describe a single event or person? Here are a few examples to start you off: diplomat/trickster; guerilla/murderer; party/junta; social democrat/red; gunman/patriot; businessman/robber; buxom/fat; brave/foolhardy; colourful/gaudy; decorative/pretentious; steadfast/obstinate; loyal/sycophantic.

Now check *The Guardian* report of 26 June 1984 (see Figure 9.2): is it completely free of bias? Visit the nearest library and look in various newspapers to find opposing accounts of a given person or event; note down the different words used in these accounts. You can then compare your lists with those of fellow students. Learn to recognise emotive words and their emotive opposites, and ask yourself what effect an account would have on you if the other words of the pair had been used.

Honest and dishonest use of emotion

Recognising that there are these pairs of emotive words does not mean condemning all emotional use of language. Emotion moves us to action; reason on the other hand only causes us to search for contrary reasons if a case is one which, emotionally, we cannot support. An appeal on behalf of starving children, or mistreated prisoners, for instance, is inevitably directed at the emotions, but may nonetheless be honest. Someone who incites a crowd to string up a suspect, however, or gets up a petition to stop a new road being built on the grounds that it will be unsafe for children, while really thinking only of the effect on himself or on the value of his house, is using emotion dishonestly. Such things occur every day, in business as well as private life. Look out for examples if you want to learn more about unbiased communication.

False argument

A device frequently used in argument, is to say event **b** happened after event **a**, therefore **b** was caused by **a**. In the Middle Ages witches were burnt at the stake on this kind of false reasoning, and today many reputations are lost and business is damaged in the same way.

Another variant of the false argument is false analogy: money flows through a business as blood flows through the body, therefore without money, business is impossible; the body must do as the head commands, therefore we must all obey the commands of our (political or other) 'leader'. Again, look out for examples of this kind of reasoning in your discussions and in your reading.

9.2 NEGOTIATION

Negotiators have to be careful in looking for arguments to support their position, not to fall into any of the verbal traps just discussed. Politicians

Fear is the legacy of temple siege

SINCE the assault on the Golden Temple, the Punjab has been virtually sealed off from the rest of India and the world. Guardian correspondent Ajoy Bose has travelled through the army-occupied province to bring out the first full reports on the troubled and angry mood of Punjabis, and their fears for the future.

THE FRAGILITY of the peace in the Punjab countryside becomes apparent even in casual conversation. Hindus and Sikhs express sharply contrasting viewpoints, indicating the deep-rooted polarisation that exists between the two communities.

Among Hindus, there is unanimous relief at the military crackdown and the death of Sant Bhindranwale and his band of extremists who had terrorised them for three months. 'Those people inside the Golden Temple were murderers and they were out to murder Hindus specially. Thank God that Indiraji had finally the sense to send the army against them,' said Hindu businessman in Chandigarh, the state capital of Punjab.

Sikhs on the other hand seem quite disoriented at the events of the past month. Their moods vary from anger and defiance to helplesness and fear, from grief and sorrow to a feeling of humiliation bristling with resentment.

'We will not forget and we will not forgive,' said Sucha Singh, an elderly Sikh peasant, member of the local council of a cluster of villages in Kapurthala district 60 mile south of Amritsar.

The peasant leader is angry about a lot of things. Like most other members of his community, he sees the army assault on the Golden Temple as the supreme insult to his faith. He is angry with the combing operations that the army and paramilitary forces have carried out in his village and the consequent arrest of many of his friends and relatives. But Sucha Singh is also disgusted with the Akali Dal leadership for leading the Sikhs to their present sorrows.

The overwhelming presence of the army underlines the tension that exists. Soldiers carrying sten guns stop and search all vehicles, including bullock carts and tractors, every few miles along the highways. Army trucks fitted with machine-guns rumble down city streets carrying soldiers with their rifles pointed suspiciously at every passer-by.

A few made the mistake of fleeing when soldiers asked them to identify themselves. Others paid with their lives for their curiosity and were shot down as suspected snipers while they sneaked upon roof tops to see the extent of damage in the Golden Temple.

The most unfortunate incident of this sort happened two days after the army had entered the temple, when troops shot dead 10 sevadars (social workers) of the famous Sikh saint, Baba Kharak Singh, in a raid in the city.

In Ropar district, a few miles from Chandigarh, angry Sikh villagers living near the Bhakra canal cut the water supply link to the neighbouring Hindu dominated state of Haryana shortly after the army entered the temple.

The Government imposed a punitive fine of 10 million rupees on the 50-odd villages around the canal, but villagers in the area are openly defiant and vow that they will not pay.

The anger and defiance of the Sikh peasantry is tempered by a sense of helplessness and fear at the superior firepower and discipline of the troops patrolling the highways.

Figure 9.2 Excerpt from *The Guardian*, 26 June 1984

and persuaders of all types use them as a matter of course, and rely on the emotion of the moment to save them from exposure. In contrast, a negotiator who uses any of these tricks will almost certainly be exposed, and once exposed will have difficulty in ever recovering his credibility.

Negotiation is an art. No-one can become a good negotiator merely by following a set of rules, firstly because all personalities are different and have to be differently used to get the best effect in negotiation, and secondly because no set of negotiations is quite like another – the personalities, issues and circumstances are always slightly different. So negotiation is an art which has to be studied and is not a routine that can be learned. It can only really be successfully developed by experience; however, clarification of the dynamics of negotiation can help us to develop our skills (see Figure 9.3).

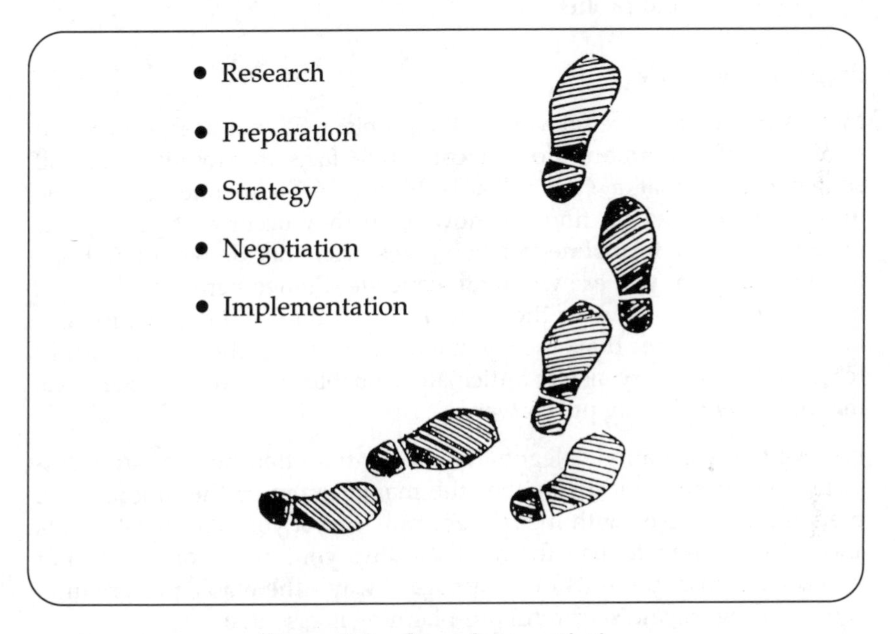

Figure 9.3 Steps in negotiation

Collecting the information

First of all get the facts straight – and make sure you have all of them – agreements, works rules, safety rules, etc. If the issue in dispute is a grievance then get information on the following:

— the people involved;

— their job classification, shifts and rates;

— the time and place of the grievance and the departments involved;

— what has been violated, ie the agreement, custom and practice, or law.

If the dispute is a wage claim, collect all the relevant information including the type of facts and arguments likely to be used by the other side and include the following:

- — movements in the cost of living and deficiencies in the price index;
- — comparisons with other workers – their earnings and rates and whether the increases were granted through Wages Councils or arbitration; the adequacy of existing rates and earnings;
- — movements in productivity (especially productivity per man hour), and the part played by the workers and by additional investment;
- — changes in the profit position of the company;
- — the likely effects of resultant price increase on the company's prospects and profits.

Preparing your case

Make sure the facts are relevant to the problem. Do not use hearsay and remember that opinions do not constitute facts in most cases, eg if someone says that a supervisor is picking on someone, define the incidences referred to, find out how often they occur and get specific instances. Before formal negotiation takes place, decide what you hope to gain and what you are willing to concede. Remember that what you hope to gain is not always the same as what you may be asked for as a negotiator. Ensure that the demands and suggestions are within reasonable limits. Try also to anticipate probable alternative suggestions that the other side may put forward.

Plan your presentation. Negotiations only too often become unnecessarily complicated because either the management or the unions have prepared their cases with insufficient care. Select your strongest points and decide when to use them, discarding your weak ones. Do not introduce your arguments in a haphazard way – the whole presentation should be logical and so careful pre-planning is essential.

You should also try to anticpate the arguments that may be put by the other side. Use your imagination if you have to describe situations of which you have not personally had experience, eg the possible effect of wage increases on the fortunes of a company or the effects of a rise in the cost of living on living standards. In doing this you should use reliable facts and not just guess at them.

Planning the strategy

The use of a strategy will help you win your case. Strategy must be planned in advance and in this timing is important. Bargain when the other side is at its weakest, for instance. The most favourable times will of course differ according to the company, the industry and the economy, eg a trade union should not plan on being tough when there is a high degree of unemployment nor an employer when there is a scarcity of good labour. Use sensible bargaining methods and try to decide on an 'acceptable' settlement well in advance, for there is always a difference between what is demanded and the final negotiated settlement.

Decide in advance on the negotiating method which best suits your personality. Are you naturally forthright, tough or conciliatory? Should you allow your natural manner full rein or adapt it to the occasion and to the people you will meet on the other side of the negotiating table? To help you decide on a negotiating style, try to find out how the other side feels about the issues.

You should also think out the consequences of various types of approach and settlement. Do not try to 'pull a fast one'. Your case should be good enough to stand on its own merits. Deception is a poor weapon and while you may gain a temporary advantage a false case may result in a wall of suspicion when next the two parties meet.

The negotiating table

— Step 1 – settle all the matters on which agreement can be reached so that you do not waste time and temper on unnecessary details. Some proposals may only need slight modification so the first efforts in bargaining are often merely exploratory.

— Step 2 – go through all the proposals; listen carefully and take note of how the other side feels about them. Try to judge the ones on which they seem to feel most strongly as well as those on which there is obvious disagreement.

— Step 3 – decide on your opening tactic carefully. Should you use a cautious start and present only part of the case or put it all in one statement? As a general rule you should, as far as is possible, keep something up your sleeve. There is no need at the outset to tell all that is known about the case; a few salient facts will often suffice.

Note on adjournments

You should always adjourn to consider any new proposals or counter proposals. Never do your thinking aloud in front of the other side, and only renew discussion when you have carefully worked out a revised plan. If, however, you have already anticipated the new move, you can carry on with the negotiation without interruption.

Try not to get bogged down in prolonged argument over one or two minor items at the beginning of bargaining. Fund out where the disagreement lies, how serious it is, and then pass on to the next point. Remember the successful bargainer is also a good listener. If either side wants only to talk and not to listen then no real bargaining can take place and there will be no basis for agreement. The art of listening and registering what is being said across the table as well as remembering the context in which key words and phrases have been employed, can mean the difference between success and failure. By doing this the bargainer can provide for snap decisions with a calculated evaluation of the intent of the other party and explore flaws in their argument.

It is important that members of the negotiating team rigidly observe the rule that they do not contradict one another during the negotiation and indeed do not speak unless asked to do so by the leader of their team. Instead make a written or whispered request for an adjournment. Do not be afraid to adjourn, it is not a sign of weakness.

Be brief and to the point. Do not just talk for the sake of talking – most negotiations are about practical matters. A business-like approach invariably ensures a quick response from the other side. Use plain language when putting a case or replying to one; this will keep the negotiation on the rails and prevent you from talking in circles.

Do not be unnecessarily tough unless you feel it is justified. In any case do not confuse toughness with noisiness. In fact as far as possible try to keep all hot-heads off the negotiation team. Lung power and bad temper are no substitute for a good case, well presented. Both sides should show the courtesy to the other that they expect themselves. This applies not only to the manner of speech but to matters of punctuality and general bearing as well. Throughout the negotiations, look for any change in the other side's attitude and be ready to alter your own to deal with them.

Ask yourself if you are making it easy for the other side to make concessions or at least to save face. Be flexible and firm. The most fair and carefully presented case may not succeed in spite of its fairness and logic. This may be because the other party remains unconvinced or is just plain stubborn. This kind of situation can be surmounted in one of two ways: by persuasion or compromise. After the less contentious or disputable proposals have been settled, those which are left are likely to require the most negotiating skill. You must decide on your priorities at this stage and know which proposals are important and which are not. You must then be ready to re-word some of the proposals where necessary. Too many negotiators are rigid and inflexible in this matter and are either unwilling or unable to modify or amend proposals – they may do this because they have left themselves too little room in which to bargain, or because they have not prepared the case with enough care.

Throughout the negotiations, try not to confuse stubborness with firmness. You should decide well in advance the minimum settlements you are willing to accept. It is often those who are most rigid and inflexible who after bitter opening argument end up discussing counter proposals after abandoning their own ideas. This is usually because the other side has been able to put forward counter proposals which are less complicated.

The wise bargainer keeps on bargaining as long as the other party continues to do so in good faith, and there appears to be a chance of a settlement. But you should not concede anything simply in order to get a settlement. There is always a reasonable point beyond which you should not be prepared to bargain and you must learn to recognise this.

After the negotiation

Always make some attempt to record the results. In order to be able to do this with confidence you must ensure throughout the bargaining that whenever a decision is made both sides are clear what it is and really do agree to it. Industrial relations is littered with examples of meetings where each side has left the negotiating table with a different impression of the result. Some of this can be considered to be deliberate but some is the result of genuine misapprehension.

At the close of negotiation the chances of further trouble are always considerably reduced if you make quite sure, at the time when the agreement is finalised, of all the details. If the last piece of business consists of a recapitulation of all the points the meeting has agreed to then few people will risk charges of breaches of faith by going back on them later. On the other hand an unstructured meeting where lots of things are said and none are recorded can lead to confusion.

Records of meetings can either be held separately by each side or, in the case of productivity bargains, for example, where there must be joint settlements, held jointly so that as few issues as possible are left only vaguely understood. Finally, make sure that both sides keep their word once an agreement is reached. Follow up the particular issues discussed a few weeks later to see that the terms of the settlement are being acted upon.

NOW TRY THIS...

It is June, the month of the annual wage negotiations in your firm, Vision Graphics. There are two main groups of employees: administrative staff (25) and technical staff (110). Administrative staff belong to the Union of Office and Allied Workers (UOAW). The UOAW is a small union with very little power to negotiate for its members. Its members are currently paid on a salary range of £4,000-£8,000. Last year they had an increase of 5%. Technical staff belong to the Union of Technical, Computing and Mechanical Operatives (UTCMO). This union has been expanding over the past five years and now has quite a powerful voice. Its members are currently paid on a salary range of £5,000-£11,000. Last year they had an increase of 5.9%.

Pay negotiations usually take place between a management team consisting of the Managing Director, Company Accountant and Personnel Manager, and a joint union team consisting of the Shop Stewards' Committee from both unions. However, this union team does not always manage to agree on a bargaining strategy before negotiations begin.

The management team base their wage negotiations on the following:

— Keeping wages below the inflation rate (over the past twelve months it has stood at 5%).

— The wages offered to comparable workers in similar industries.

— The end-of-year financial figures of the company.

All of the above figures are also available to union negotiators.

The union team base their wage negotiations on the following:

The Administrative Union

— Keeps abreast of the inflation rate.

— Seeks to raise their pay more in line with the technical staff.

The Technical Union

— Keeps abreast of the inflation rate.

— Seeks to raise the pay level in line with their competitor company, Graphlinks Ltd (where salaries are between £5,500 and £12,500).

— The administrative staff use the same canteen as management, but the technical staff have their own. The technical staff therefore feel they are discriminated against, especially as they are often served chips, whereas in the other canteen more 'healthy' food is offered.

— For the last two years some women in the UOAW have put in a plea for a crèche to be made available for the use of their children. Their union may decide to push this demand further this year.

— Both unions also want a shorter working week of 38 hours. See Table.

Table 9.1 Recent wage settlements in comparable industries

Firm	Month settled	% increase	New salary scale administrative staff	New salary scale technical staff
Comptec Ltd	May	6.0	£4,600 – £8,700	£5,800 – £12,250
Graphlinks Ltd	March	5.4	£4,500 – £8,500	£5,500 – £12,500
Systems Go	Feb	5.0	£4,300 – £8,000	£5,300 – £11,000

Table 9.2 The weekly working hours for the past five years

Company	1986	1985	1984	1983	1982
Vision Graphics	39½	39½	40	40	40
Comptec Ltd	38½	39	39½	40	40
Graphlinks Ltd	38	39	39½	40	40
Systems Go	39	39½	39½	39½	40

Graphlinks Ltd is the most comparable to Vision Graphics in terms of location, size and production line. Comptec has had a great deal of government money invested in its initial growth stages which makes it a rather unusual company.

Pay increases over the past five years:

Vision Graphics	54%
Comptec Ltd	66%
Graphlinks Ltd	59%
Systems Go	51%

Analysis

In the light of the information gathered by the management team, the personnel director has to do four things:

— Assess the case the union is likely to make.

— Estimate the initial claim arising from that case and what the union may be prepared to settle for.

— Set out the case the company should make in reply to the union claim.

— Recommend the negotiating strategy to be used by the company.

Exercise

Working in groups, prepare either the union case or the management case. Now, using the cases prepared, role-play the negotiations.

HUMAN COMMUNICATION

SAMPLE PAPER - NEW SYLLABUS

CANDIDATES SHOULD ATTEMPT ANY FIVE QUESTIONS ONLY

(Future papers will specify a compulsory first question. Candidates will then choose another four questions which they wish to attempt).

Time 3 : hours

Clearly cross out 'surplus' answers

Failure to do this will result in only the first 5 answers being marked

No reference material of any kind may be taken into the examination

Answer Five questions only
All questions carry equal marks

(Note: in future Question 1 will be a compulsory question. Candidates will then choose a further four questions to answer) .

Question 1

a) Describe two methods which the management of a large organisation can use to communicate important messages to their workforce.

10 marks

b) Discuss the relative advantages and disadvantages of these two methods as ways of ensuring effective communication and developing good relationships between management and workforce.

10 marks

Question 2

You have seen an advertisement for a Junior Programmer with a firm called Atlas Computing Limited. The advertisement states that a written application should be made to the Personnel Manager, but gives no indication of what form your application should take.

a) State, with reasons, the format or layout which you would consider to be suitable for such an application

8 marks

AND

b) Write an application which you consider will be most effective. You may invent any necessary details.

12 marks

Question 3

Read the following passage and answer the questions below:

The Flexible Time-Clock

Flexible working hours is a system which, by putting an end to the nine to five working day myth, brings a more human touch to the working situation, but does not force anybody into another straitjacket. It does not demand, either, that the individual, who is set in his or her ways, should change their habits. With flexible working hours, the working day is split into three sections - one when everyone must be present (the core time) and two at either end of the day (the flexible bands) when everyone can come and go as (s)he pleases.

It is now estimated that there are well over 2,000 applications of the system. It has been adopted in administrative organisations, retailing, insurance companies, and head offices, as well as in local and central government.

In the system core times are set to coincide with the daily peak demands on the organisation – in an office from 10am until 4pm and flexible bands are added during which employees can be present or not at their will. In the office situation, these might well be between 8am and 10am and 4pm and 6.30pm. The main restrictions, apart from presence during the core time, is that over a given settlement period, which can be a week or a fortnight, but more usually a month, employees have to work the total number of hours for which they have contracted, ie if the contracted time is seven hours per day, they have to be present in total for 140 hours in a month of 20 working days. There are refinements. Many companies have added an additional flexible band to cover the lunch break. Employees can take up to 1.5 hours, but they must observe a minimum of half-an-hour. Most companies which have implemented this system allow a further concession; the possibility of a debit or credit carry forward of up to ten hours. Debit/credit hours should be made up, or taken, during the flexible bands of the following settlement period; but some companies allow a half day per month off in core time against accumulated credit hours.

It is not all 'blue skies' however. Nor has the old adage that if you give a man enough rope he will hang himself proved true, either. In a typical firm, employees are almost always in credit to the tune of, on average, approximately four hours per employee. Also there are other advantages to the company.

Out of a total of thirty companies replying, to a questionnaire, improvement in working atmosphere was reported by 24; reduction of paid absence by 25; reduction of overtime worked by 15; increased productivity by individuals adjusting hours worked to their own best work rhythm by 17; improved recruitment success by 19; and reduced personnel turnover by 6.

Extract from Management Today

a) Summarise in not more than 100 words how the flexible work-hours system works. **8 marks**

b) What advantages does the system have
   (i) for employers **4 marks**
   (ii) for employees? **4 marks**

c) What disadvantages can you foresee? **4 marks**

Question 4

The Managing Director of your company has been on a tour of the complex and has been annoyed to discover that in the foundry unit he saw workers blatantly ignoring the safety regulations - the non-wearing of safety glasses and protective headgear was the most common.

a) Draft a memo to deal with this problem and state to whom the memo should be distributed. **8 marks**

b) Write a report to the Managing Director recommending measures you would wish to take to improve safety standards in the complex. **12 marks**

You may invent any information or detail necessary to enable you to write the memo and report.

Question 5

Your employer has requested that you, as Office Manager, inform the new Office Juniors on the importance of good telephone technique.

a) Write a memo to all new entrants on how they should answer the telephone, and include as much advice as you can give on a good telephone manner. **12 marks**

b) Design a telephone message form with appropriate headings to help those taking calls to record all necessary details. **8 marks**

Question 6

You are shortly to be interviewed for a post as a computer programmer. What preparations can you make beforehand and what action can you take during the interview to ensure as far as possible a favourable impression? **20 marks**

Question 7

A firm is considering computerisation. You have been retained as their consultant to implement the project. Management fully support this proposal but some of the staff are a little apprehensive. You have been asked to give a speech to all the employees on the benefits of computerisation in order to obtain their full co-operation. Describe how you would go about preparing the speech, what points you would include and what factors you would keep in mind about delivery. **20 marks**

Question 8

Meetings play a vital part in the running of any organisation.

a) Discuss some of the reasons why they are so important. **12 marks**

b) Describe some of the characteristics of an effective meeting. **8 marks**

SAMPLE PAPER

'Guidance Notes'

Question 1

This question sets out to answer a candidate's ability to 'understand the relationship between the structure of an organisation and the dissemination of information' (Chapter 7) . Part A of the question requires students to identify two effective channels of downward vertical communication in a large organisation and describe them. These might include notices and posters, meetings, home journals and bulletins, pay packet inserts, letters and memo's etc. Part A carries 10 marks. Part B of the question, which also carries 10 marks, asks candidates to discuss the relative advantages and disadvantages of the methods chosen in terms of their overall effectiveness. Answers to this part of the question should include an appraisal of their feedback potential, cost factors, practical implications, employee perception of appropriateness, etc.

Question 2

This question asks candidates to decide on the most effective format or layout when responding to a job advertisement. Part A, which carries 8 marks, requires candidates to recognise that current practice dictates that this will be a curriculum vitae or data-sheet (sometimes referred to in certain countries as a bio-data) , or some other form of schematic layout accompanied by a letter in support of the application. The answer to Part B, which carries 12 marks, requires a covering letter with an appropriate layout conforming to the conventions of letter writing (4 marks) and a curriculum vitae (or alternative schematic layout) . The CV will be comprehensive, attractive to the recipient, clearly and logically ordered, etc, (8 marks) . This part of the syllabus is covered by Chapters 3 and 5.

Question 3

It is the intention of this question to test candidates' ability to summarise and interpret written information. Part A requires candidates to display the skills of analysis and synthesis in summarising a passage on flexible work-hours. The summary should include reference to the four main features of the system which are flexibility, the concept of core-time, the scheme's widespread adoption and a recognition that the scheme can be advantageous to both employers and employees. This part carries 8 marks. Part B, which also carries 8 marks, is divided into two sections. The first section, carrying 4 marks, asks candidates to identify from the passage the advantages which the system offers for employers. These should include reduced paid absence, reduced overtime (payments) , increased productivity, improved recruitment and reduced staff turnover. The second section of Part B, which also carries 4 marks, seeks an identification of the advantages or the system for employees. These should include enhanced flexibility, the improved working atmosphere and the opportunity for time-off. The final part of the question, Part C, requires candidates to extract from the passage the disadvantages of flexible work-hours. To gain the full 4 marks, candidates should refer to the financial cost, the administrative costs (time/organisation) and the problems which management are likely to encounter in introducing the scheme (problems of managing 'change') .

Question 4

This question, which is in two parts, sets out to test candidates abilities in respect of memorandum and report writing. Part A of the question carries 8 marks. The memo should be sent to *all* production personnel (2 marks) observe the conventions of layout (2 marks) and should clearly and concisely remind all workers of the need to familiarise themselves with the safety regulations and adhere to them. Reference should be made to safety glasses and protective headgear as examples (4 marks) . Part B of the question requires a brief formal report. Two (2) marks are allocated for the initial layout and 4 marks for an appropriate, logical and clear schematic organisation of the body of the report. The content should be accurate, comprehensive and well expressed in a factual manner. The style should be formal and the vocabulary appropriate, (4 marks) . The final 2 marks are allocated for overall neatness of presentation. Report and memorandum writing skills are dealt with in Chapter 3.

Question 5

This question is concerned with the use of the telephone, the design of appropriate forms and with drafting memoranda. These topics are covered in chapters 3 and 4. Part A is worth 12 marks, 4 of which are allocated to the adoption of an appropriate layout for the memorandum. The other 8 marks are awarded for the content of the memo which should give sound and comprehensive advice on a good telephone manner. Points referred to should include the need to answer promptly giving the name of the firm, the need to inform the caller of the action you are taking, the need for courtesy at all times and the importance of recording calls intended for colleagues. This final point is examined more fully in Part B of this question which requires candidates to design a telephone message form. The 8 marks awarded to part B are apportioned as 6 marks for the comprehensiveness of the form and a further 2 marks for the neatness and appropriateness of its design.

Question 6

Understanding the features and demands of job interviews and being able to perform competently both as an interviewer and interviewee are addressed by this question. This has always been a part of the syllabus which students' have regarded as very relevant and applicable and it has attracted some outstandingly good work over a long period of time. Twelve (12) marks are allocated to that part of the students answer which covers interview preparation. Thus, reference to a letter confirming intention to attend, undertaking research into the organisation and if possible the specific post, the need for preparation of answers to anticipated questions, the need for attention to appearance, punctuality, etc, will all be rewarded. 8 marks are retained for that part of the candidates answer which refers to the actual conduct of the interview. Candidates should recognise in their answers that a favourable impression will be created by a pleasant manner, appropriate dress and appearance, evidence of preparation for the interview, confidence, enthusiasm, technical knowledge, willingness to ask questions, etc (Chapter 6).

Question 7

This question contains presentation skills and marks are awarded for details of data collection strategies (5 marks) pre-planning the order and sequence, use of visual aids, etc (5 marks), the practical considerations relating to venue, seating, lighting, etc (5 marks) and finally for aspects of delivery such as style and tone and emphasis upon the need for the presentation to be reassuring (5 marks) (Chapter 4) .

Question 8

Part A of this question, (12 marks) , asks students to identify the reasons why business meetings are so very important in the effective running of organisations. These include their role in giving and receiving information, coordinating, airing grievances, negotiation, problem solving, innovation, decision making etc. A further 8 marks are allocated to Part B which concerns the characteristics of effective meetings. These include the importance of thorough preparation, the need for clear aims to be shared by all participants, a recognition of potential barriers to progress, control through effective chairpersonship and an awareness of the problems of appropriate size and composition (Chapter 8) .

Further Reading

Little P, *Communication at work*, Pitman, 1987

Peel M, *Improving your communication skills*, Kogan Page, 1990

Robinson D, Power R, *Spotlight on communication*, Pitman, 1984

Smithson S, Whitehead J, *Business communication*, Croner Publications, 1987

Woolcott L A, Unwin W R, *Communication for business and secretarial students*, 2nd edition, Macmillan, 1979

Index